guide to wine

guide to wine

AN INTRODUCTION
FOR BEGINNERS

Fiona Sims

p

To Mark and Birdy

This is a Parragon Publishing Book
This edition published in 2003

Parragon Publishing
Queen Street House
4 Queen Street
Bath BA1 1HE
United Kingdom

ISBN: 0-75256-485-4

Printed in China

Produced by The Bridgewater Book Company Ltd,
Lewes, East Sussex, United Kingdom

Creative Director **Terry Jeavons**
Art Director **Emily Wilkinson**
Editorial Director **Fiona Biggs**
Senior Editor **Mark Truman**
Editorial Assistant **Tom Kitch**
Photographer **Calvey Taylor-Haw**
Picture Researcher **Lynda Marshall**
Maps **Richard Constable, Lorraine Harrison**
Models **Matthew Birch, I. Kaskero**

Contents

Introduction

Wine appreciation isn't the preserve of the elite any more. Wine is classless, affordable and at a store near you. And guess what? We, the wine drinkers, can take some of the credit for this. If we weren't prepared to try new things, winemakers wouldn't bother making them.

The world is the wine drinker's oyster—or should that be bottle? The choice of wine on offer has never been so good, with the shelves in our supermarkets and wine shops groaning under the weight—and it's getting bigger every year. And at very reasonable prices. There's plenty of decent stuff to drink even at low prices. Bad wine, in fact, is almost extinct.

On top of all that, the scientists have confirmed what the Ancient Greeks knew all along, that wine is good for you—in moderation, of course. It's a happy situation—and it's getting happier.

So much has changed even in the last ten years. Take Australia, for example. Australian wine was a novelty in the late 1980s, when we drank mostly French, German, and Italian wine. But now Australia is number two in the market, roaring past Germany and way ahead of Italy.

There's a new world of wine out there, a world without châteaus or communes, where the grape variety rules, where the taste of the fruit and the name of the grape are what matters most. Armed with their shiny new equipment and the latest ideas, New World producers make vibrant, juicy, ripe wines, with the grape variety on the label. It's a language that everybody can now understand.

The Old World has wised up. They've realized that maybe the old ways are not always the best, after all. Offspring are scrubbing up their parents' cellars, installing stainless steel tanks and making wines that are ready to drink now—none of this ten-year-wait business. They're opening up to criticism, and listening to the fast techno-talking newcomers, some of whom roam Europe, transforming attitudes and inexpensive wine.

So much more is known now about how to get the vineyard ripe every year, and how to make the best out of it when the weather doesn't comply. Then there's the huge amount of scientific know-how that goes into establishing a grape's sugar levels, acid, tannin, color and flavor, and the transformation of those grapes into wine.

Although some fogies warn that all wine will eventually taste the same—the so-called "Stepford Wines"—these modern methods allow producers to get the best out of their grapes and their land. The more switched-on are able to express the subtle nuances of a particular vineyard in their wines, a particular corner of the vineyard, even.

That's not meant to sound scary. You really can taste the difference sometimes—honest! You just need a bit of confidence, and that confidence comes with knowledge.

That's where *Guide to Wine* comes in. The book has been written for those who are just getting into wine and who want to know the basics—to help you get your bearings in the vinous jungle. It will get you moving confidently around the shelves of your local supermarket or liquor store, and ordering wine in restaurants without embarrassment.

First stop is flavor. The book shows you how to taste and offers an insight into the different grapes and their different styles, sorting the plummy Merlots from the blackcurranty Cabernets.

And if you're wondering what to serve for a wedding, or with your Friday night takeaway curry or Tex-Mex, the book has the answer. It'll also steer you around any tricky wine-busting ingredients, and show you where to buy wine —from cyberspace to the specialist merchant.

There's practical stuff, too, on using the correct glassware (yes, it does make a difference), how to decipher wine labels and how to spot a corked wine. And before you start stashing your new booty in the kitchen near the fridge or the stove (you can stop that right now), there's information on how to store wine correctly.

A whistle-stop tour of the world's vineyards highlights what makes wines different, and which grapes are grown where. It also sheds some light on the often arcane wine classification systems in use in many of Europe's vineyards.

It finishes up among the stainless steel in the winery. This may seem a little geeky, but understanding a bit more about how wine is made will help bring about the confidence to relax and enjoy it.

Fact: the more you taste, the more you'll learn. So don't just reach for that bottle of Australian Chardonnay or Chilean Cabernet you keep buying. Go for something else—anything else—and get tasting.

getting
into grapes

Flavor is the first thing that springs to mind when you're choosing a

bottle of wine. And it's the grape variety that tells you most of all

what flavor you're going to get. There are hundreds of grape

varieties out there, but just a few—about nine, in fact—that make

most of the wines on our shelves, so get reading. But first, pucker

up and learn how to taste. All that curious swirling, sucking, spitting

you see wine buffs doing at wine-tastings does have a purpose, and,

with a bit of practice, you too can hit the spittoon in one.

How to Taste

The more wines you try, the more you'll develop your palate—it's as simple as that. And how you try them makes all the difference. I know that all that curious slurping you see wine tasters doing at a tasting looks highly mysterious, but it's not. Swirl, sniff, and spit, that's all it is. But why do you swirl? What are you supposed to be looking for exactly? What is tannin? What is acidity?

The first step is to fill your glass until it's about a third full. Have a good look at it. Tilt it slightly against a white background, or hold it up to the daylight so you can see the range of colors from the center to the rim. Older red wines start to fade at the rim, with a browny, tawny color. Red wines from hotter climates and gutsier red grape varieties have the deepest colors.

Now give it a swirl, getting a good motion going. This releases all the wine's aromas. Jam your nose right into the glass and inhale slowly. Your first impressions are the most vivid. After two or three sniffs, your senses are neutralized. An experienced taster will be able to tell a lot from just inhaling: what grape variety it is, even where the wine comes from. A novice will soon start to spot the key fruit flavors that indicate a particular grape variety.

When you inhale, think of those aromas you get in terms of flavors that are familiar to you. It'll take a few goes to get the hang of it—but once you do, you'll soon be smelling warm cocoa, freshly mown grass, even peach melba. It doesn't matter if you're the only one who gets those particular aromas; everybody has their own flavor references and, anyway, that's part of the fun.

Now for the tasting. Take a good sip and roll it around. The reason those experts make such a noise once the wine is in their mouths is that they are trying to reach every part of their tongue: sweetness at the tip; saltiness a little farther back and sourness, or acidity, at the sides, with bitterness sensed at the very back. Make a note of any acidity, sweetness, or toughness. It helps if you suck in some air through your lips, because it kick-starts the aromas and flavors. Now give it a good chew.

Scribble down your first impressions. Some flavors are more obvious than others

left Fill the glass only a third full so that you can inhale all the wine's aromas.

at first, but don't worry too much about finding a garden of fruit flavors—it'll come. Think about the weight in the mouth. Is it light, medium, or full-bodied? Is it balanced? What are the levels of acidity, alcohol, dryness/sweetness, fruit flavor, and tannin? Then swallow—or spit, if you have many more to taste. Make a note of any lingering flavors (known as the length). Do you like it?

Things to look out for when you're tasting wine

Acidity

Makes the wine taste crisp and fresh. Too much and it will taste unpleasantly sharp and bitter. Not enough and it will taste flabby.

Alcohol

Obviously this is found in all wine, but the higher the level of alcohol gets, the rounder the wine feels in the mouth. If it's out of balance with the fruit and tannin and so on, then it will feel hot, too—like a dash of Tabasco.

above Take a sip and swirl the wine around your mouth to reach all parts of your tongue, even if you do make strange noises.

Dryness/Sweetness

This is affected by the amount of natural sugar in a wine. Sweetness needs to be balanced by acidity or the wine is too cloying. Don't confuse dryness with acidity, however—a very dry wine such as fino sherry can in fact be quite low in acidity.

Fruit

Let your imagination run wild and prepare yourself—wine doesn't smell and taste of grapes. Instead, flavors can resemble a whole garden of fruit, or chocolate, cigars, nuts, coffee, or even rising bread dough.

Tannin

Tannin creates that furry, drying feeling that you get in the mouth after a swig of a very young red. It comes from the stalks, pips, and skins of grapes. Tannin helps with the weight of a wine and softens with age.

The Big White Grapes

left Wine made from the Chardonnay grape ranks among the most popular in the world. The grapes grow just as easily in the heat of California and the Pacific as in their native eastern France.

in the United States with white wine, Chardonnay also dominates the Australian wine industry with its rich, blowsy style.

What does it taste like?

At best, Chardonnay produces complex aromas of nuts, butter, toast, and mushrooms with tastes that range from apple and lemon through to peach and melon, with the same buttery, creamy, nutty notes suggested by the wine's aromas. It's wonderfully easy to grow, and is as happy in the cooler climates of its homeland Burgundy as it is in the hot climate of California's Central Coast.

Chardonnay loves oak, and winemakers the world over have discovered that fiddling around with Chardonnay in oak (whether in a barrel, or in contact with oak chips or staves) can mimic the richness that classic white Burgundy takes years to acquire.

It blends well with less pronounced varieties, though the greatest Chardonnays are all unblended.

Chardonnay

A name so familiar to wine drinkers that many of us don't realize that it is, in fact, a grape variety. Or that it is the grape that is responsible for another global wine drinkers' favorite—Chablis.

Where is it grown?

Chardonnay has traveled the world with unrivaled success, producing, at worst, drinkable wines almost everywhere it lays down roots—from British Columbia to the British Isles, from India to Uruguay. Only Portugal seems to have withstood Chardonnay mania. Now synonymous

Sauvignon Blanc

Sancerre, Pouilly-Fumé, and Fumé Blanc are still the mainstays of fashionable bars from San Francisco to London, but many of us don't know that they are made from Sauvignon Blanc.

Where is it grown?

This classic variety has been grown in France for centuries, from the Gironde to the Loire Valley and, when blended with Sémillon, is responsible for the delectable sweet whites of Sauternes and Barsac. It is only in the last 20 years or so that it has become popular in the world's newer wine regions, where it turns out wines of varying flavours—if still easily recognizable.

What does it taste like?

Cat's pee on a gooseberry bush is an oft-quoted description, used readily in New Zealand's Marlborough region, where Sauvignon Blanc shines. In the warmer climate wine regions of California, Chile, and Australia, Sauvignon Blanc tends toward the dry, soft, and creamy, which can turn flabby. South Africa excels in the grape, especially in its cooler regions of Constantia and Elgin, and you can add freshly squeezed grapefruit and limes to the flavor spectrum.

below Carefully hand-picking Riesling grapes, which form the basis of many of Germany's greatest dry white wines.

Riesling

First up, it's pronounced *reece-ling*, not *rye-sling*. Riesling is one of the most mispronounced grapes and is not to be confused with Welschriesling, or Italian Riesling, which are quite unrelated varieties. But the very same grape as Johannisberg Riesling and Rhine Riesling. It's also one of the most undervalued grapes. It's still a hard sell in restaurants and supermarkets, yet it produces some of the finest dry white wines (and some serious sweet wine) in the world.

Where it is grown?

Most Riesling comes from Germany. It reflects the different soils and microclimates in which it is grown without losing its identity better than almost any other grape, from the steely styles of the Saar to the oily, pungent wines of the Pfalz, as well as scaling heights over the border in Alsace.

It's an early ripening grape that is suited to these cooler areas of Germany and Alsace, but it's now also planted all over the southern hemisphere—to great effect in Australia, whose warmer climate gives the wines a more limey, exotic fruit character.

What does it taste like?

Riesling is extraordinarily aromatic, with flavors ranging from all manner of fruits to honey, minerals, a garden center full of flowers and, distinctly, gasoline (a good thing). Riesling has enormous aging potential—a 20-year-old still turns heads.

Sémillon

One of the unsung heroes of white wine production in France, Sémillon is a key ingredient in Bordeaux, in sweet Sauternes, and in the nearby Graves.

above A windmill stands guard over Chenin Blanc vineyards in the Loire Valley, as the grapes ripen under a clear blue sky.

Where is it grown?

Unblended, Sémillon positively shines in Australia, notably the Hunter Valley, and is Chile's second most planted white grape after Sauvignon Blanc. Even New Zealand is having a go.

What does it taste like?

The variety is often blended with Chardonnay. On its own, Sémillon can be fairly neutral, but when grown in certain areas, picked at a certain ripeness, and made in a certain way, with a bit of barrel fermentation, it can go 20 years or more. It can produce deliciously lemony dry whites in France, while in Australia you tend to get something altogether more rich and waxy, giving off big butterscotch aromas when aged.

Chenin Blanc

One of the world's most versatile grape varieties. At its best, Chenin Blanc is capable of producing some of the finest sweet wines in the world with great aging potential.

Where is it grown?

In France, Chenin Blanc is grown predominantly in the central part of the Loire Valley. Elsewhere, it dominates the white wine scene in South Africa, where it turns out dry, refreshingly crisp, though sometimes rather bland, whites. It is prolific in California, where it often ends up as a nondescript base for everyday, reasonably crisp whites of varying degrees of sweetness.

What does it taste like?

The dry version can produce wines of great intensity, with aromas and tastes from apples and apricots to honey and straw. It makes fair volumes of sparkling, too, though not as remarkable.

Other Great White Grapes

Aligoté

Burgundy's second white grape (to Chardonnay). In good years, on Burgundy's best slopes and on the poorest soils, Aligoté can produce a decent bottle of wine. It's great in Kir (white wine with a splash of crème de cassis). It's popular in Eastern Europe, where its high acidity is prized in Bulgaria and Romania. It is also Russia's second most planted white wine grape, and can be found in Chile and California.

Colombard

Don't expect too much from Colombard. This handy variety is widely planted in southwest France for distilling into Cognac and Armagnac, and in France rarely goes beyond the crisp, grassy freshness of a Côtes de Gascogne. In California, South Africa and Australia, however, the hot sun encourages pungent, tropical fruit flavors.

Gewürztraminer

The most distinctly aromatic of grapes, the pink-skinned Gewürztraminer is grown in Germany, Austria, northern Italy, Eastern Europe, and a few New World countries. One sniff, and recognition is instant: lychees, roses, even ginger and cinnamon (*Gewürz* means spice). It is at its most exotic in Alsace, where it has three main styles: dry, medium sweet (*Vendange Tardive*) and lusciously sweet (*Sélection des Grains Nobles*), but is showing promise in the cooler climes of the southern hemisphere.

Grüner Veltliner

This is Austria's big white grape and it ranges from an inoffensive white from the Weinviertel, in lower Austria, to a serious wine from the best spots in the Wachau. Its sappy, pungent fruit makes it an ideal partner for a whole range of foods.

Marsanne

This meaty, low-acid white hails from the northern Rhône, where it has all but taken over from its traditional blending partner Roussanne. Marsanne has become increasingly popular all over the world, and in Australia produces hefty, dry whites packed with honeysuckle and mango fruits.

below Traditionally, in its native Rhône valley, Roussanne is blended with Marsanne, but is an increasingly popular variety on its own in California.

left The classic Muscat Blanc à Petits Grains, growing in Beaumes-de-Venise, produces the most grape-tasting wine in the world.

The Muscats

A huge family of vines, the Muscats range from the light, elegant, rose-scented Alsace Muscat to the sweet, refreshing, low-alcohol fizz that is Moscato d'Asti. Then there are the Australian liqueur Muscats, the Spanish Moscatels and the *vins doux naturels* Muscats from the south of France, such as Beaumes-de-Venise.

The Pinots

Namely, Pinot Blanc and Pinot Gris. Pinot Blanc has similar buttery, appley fruit to a light, unoaked Chardonnay. It is flexible with food and is at its most flavorsome in Alsace and Austria. Another source of good, dry Pinot Blanc is Germany, particularly in the Pfalz and Baden, and northeast Italy.

Pinot Blanc is a white mutation of Pinot Gris, an increasingly fashionable variety that makes everything from bone dry to richly sweet wine. Pinot Blanc is planted throughout central and eastern Europe and as far south as northern Italy (light, neutral Pinot Grigio). The best comes from Alsace, but Germany, Austria, and Switzerland do pretty well with Pinot Gris. Outside the old world, Oregon has shown the most interest in the grape, where it produces lightly honeyed, dry wines.

Melon de Bourgogne

Better known as Muscadet, the grape that makes this famous dry Loire white—grown virtually nowhere else—is often mistakenly known by the wine's regional name. Melon de Bourgogne is a pretty neutral grape, but it has enough acidity and whiff of the sea to partner shellfish beautifully. Given contact with its lees (*sur lie*) it gives off an appealingly crisp, lemony aroma, with a pleasantly nutty finish.

Müller-Thurgau

The bane of Germany, Müller-Thurgau is a boring crossing of Riesling and Silvaner, much used in cheap, sweetish German blends—and thankfully on the wane. It does have a few high points, though: a handful of Italians in the Alto Adige have managed to extract some palatable fruit, as have the Swiss—and, of course, it is England's most planted variety, where it can sometimes produce crisp, medium-dry whites.

Roussanne

Another catwalk grape, and Marsanne's blending partner, this Rhône-born grape has an unforgettable aroma – almost feral, with ripe stone fruits, citrus, and hay flavors. As one of the four grape varieties allowed into white Châteauneuf-du-Pape, it is mostly blended, but it is increasingly star-ring on its own in California's Central Coast.

Scheurebe

Another German crossing, thought to be a Silvaner x Riesling, Scheurebe is a tad more interesting than Müller-Thurgau. It produces sweet grapes, but keeps its acidity, and is easily affected by botrytis—which means it can produce the extremely fine sweet white Beerenauslese and Trockenbeerenauslese wines. Austria dabbles with the grape, too, where it is known as Sämling 88.

Silvaner

Or Sylvaner. This is another German grape that stays mostly in its native country or parts of central Europe. It was big in Germany in the first half of the twentieth century, and still shines in Franken, where the best Silvaners come from. About half Germany's Silvaner grapes are planted in the Rheinhessen—the world's Silvaner capital.

Torrontés

Argentina's great white hope, Torrontés produces spicy, dry, refreshing whites. It started life in Galicia, northwest Spain, where it is still found in the white wines of Ribeiro.

Verdelho

This Portuguese variety takes center stage in Australia, where it makes vibrant, tangy, full-bodied dry wines, particularly in the Hunter Valley in New South Wales, and in some of the hotter Australian regions. In fact, it is regarded by some as the classic white grape of McLaren Vale, in South Australia.

Viognier

Until recently, this heady, aromatic, low-yielding variety from the northern Rhône had little competition, but worthy contenders are pouring out of cellars from California to the cooler areas of Australia. Its spiritual home, though, will always be the Rhône appellation of Condrieu, where it jumps from blossom to stone fruit aromas.

Ugni Blanc (Trebbiano)

Not the most exciting of grapes, but Ugni Blanc is so widely grown that it can't be ignored. It crops up in Vin de Pays des Côtes de Gascogne, and in the Languedoc. In Italy—as Trebbiano—it makes neutral whites: Soave, Frascati, and Orvieto. Its lack of flavor means it is often blended or used in brandy production.

below The Pinot Blanc grape is a white mutation of Pinot Gris and produces all kinds of wine from bone dry to richly sweet.

The Big Red Grapes

Cabernet Sauvignon

Arguably the world's most famous grape, Cabernet Sauvignon is grown just about everywhere there are vineyards.

Where is it grown?
From its power base in Bordeaux, where it is almost always blended, it has been snapped up by other regions in France, and across much of the vinous globe. Some blend it with their own native varieties, others bottle it on its own.

What does it taste like?
Even with a dollop of other grapes mixed in, and the change of soil and climate, the Cabernet Sauvignon grape still manages to retain its character—with its powerful blackcurrant aroma, you can spot a

Cabernet at fifty paces. Of course, there are many variations: Australia and New Zealand, for example, place more emphasis on soft, vanilla-laced fruit in their Cabernets; Chile, meanwhile, goes for juicy plum and blackcurrants, and California has developed a monster style all of its own. Even the Lebanon wants to join in.

Merlot

Fat and juicy and not too tannic, Merlot has universal appeal.

Where is it grown?
Wine buffs sigh at the mention of Merlot on Bordeaux's right bank. It takes center stage in St Emilion and Pomerol, where it turns out serious wines with serious price tags, nudging growers the world over to try and replicate their efforts. It is still the most widely planted grape variety in Bordeaux, where it softens the edges of Cabernet Sauvignon. It is widely grown in the south of France for *vins de pays* and it is big in South Africa, Australia, and New Zealand. Merlot has also been making waves in the United States in recent years, where it has become the red answer to Chardonnay.

What does it taste like?
Black cherries, blackcurrants, plums, vanilla, toffee, and spice, although US Merlot is quite a different animal, with lots of dense,

left With their instantly recognizable blackcurrant aroma, Cabernet Sauvignon grapes are grown just about wherever wine is made and are the basis of many great reds.

What does it taste like?

At its best, Pinot Noir combines a gamut of fruit and flavor—roses and raspberries, cherries and cranberries, truffles and well-hung game—with a texture that is extraordinarily silky.

Syrah (Shiraz)

Another grape with bags of personality and loads of flavor, Syrah—known as Shiraz in Australia—makes world-class wines.

tannic, chocolatey fruit. The Chileans do well with the grape, too, extracting soft, plummy fruit, as does Argentina.

Pinot Noir

A real charmer, Pinot Noir prompts even the most conservative wine drinker to spew flowery adjectives and it is the Holy Grail for many winemakers.

Where is it grown?

The best site is Burgundy's Côte d'Or, where it becomes more scented and exotic with age. France's other Pinot Noir areas include the Loire, Alsace and, of course, Champagne, where it's used as a blending wine in bubbly. Outside France, Germany through to Romania have had fair success with the variety, but it's not the easiest grape to grow. It's thin-skinned and early ripening, and more sensitive than most to the climate (too cold and the wine is dilute, too warm and you get jelly), but pick a good spot to grow Pinot Noir and away you go. In the New World they are still experimenting with various sites, but they've got it figured out in certain areas of California's Central Coast and it doesn't do too badly around Carneros. Oregon is having a successful time with the grape, while New Zealand is the most important southern hemisphere product.

Where is it grown?

Its home is the northern Rhône, site of two of the world's greatest reds—Hermitage and Côte-Rôtie. It is Australia's most planted red variety, and excels in regions like the Barossa and Eden Valley. In California, it has a hallowed following—slaves to Syrah are called "Rhône Rangers." South Africa is making waves with the grape, although it is still early days. Other pockets of Europe —such as Italy and Spain—are also having a go, while South America and New Zealand are beginning to shine.

What does it taste like?

Blackberry, damson and plum fruits, a whiff of smoke, a hint of chocolate and an occasional blast of violets. Its general liveliness means it blends well with other varieties, such as sweeter Grenache and muddier Mourvèdre, as it is in the southern Rhône. In Australia, it blends well with blackcurranty Cabernet Sauvignon, but it shines on its own, with its chocolate, vanilla, and molasses nose.

Other Great Red Grapes

Barbera

A native of northwest Italy, Barbera vies with Sangiovese as the most widely planted red grape in the country. It is low in tannin and high in acidity and, if grown for high yields, produces bright, fruity "quaffers." Keep the yields down (as top estates in the Piedmont do) and you get intensely rich wines. Add oak, and you've got a stunner. Grown in Argentina and California, too.

Cabernet Franc

Cabernet Sauvignon's parent—though you wouldn't know it. When grown in its ideal cool climate, the wine Cabernet Franc produces is much lighter, with a grassy freshness. In Bordeaux, it is blended with Merlot and it thrives in the Loire Valley. It is widely grown in northern Italy—particularly in Friuli and the Alto Adige. It is showing promise, too, in Washington State and on California's North Coast. Even the South Africans and Australians are having a go.

Dolcetto

A bit of fun, Dolcetto. It's a low acid alternative to mouth-puckering Barbera, with lively purple, plum fruit and is virtually exclusive to Piedmont. It's best drunk within a year or two, but some clever producers manage to make it taste better by aging it for a time in the bottle.

Gamay

Ever wondered what grape went into Beaujolais Nouveau? Well, it's Gamay, which is a great quaffer. It is low in tannins and stuffed with juicy fruit. The Beaujolais producers get this easy fruit with carbonic maceration—a technique that they have widely adopted (see page 159). It does get serious, in the Beaujolais Crus (such as Morgon), and will even age a bit.

Grenache

Another "glugger," Grenache is known as Garnacha in Spain and is grown across great tracts of southern France, Spain, and Sardinia, as well as in California and Australia. The best are light in color, with rich, raspberry fruit. It bulks out the wines of Rioja, where it is blended with Tempranillo, and forms the base of the southern French sweet wines (*vins doux naturels*) of Banyuls and Maury.

left One of the world's most widely planted grapes, Grenache produces what are known as "quaffing" rather than great wines, popular where wine-drinking is a daily staple.

above Best-known for Californian light blush wine, Zinfandel is also responsible for powerfully aromatic and much finer dry reds.

Malbec

This is Argentina's big red grape. It is also found in the southwest of France, Australia, California, South Africa, and Italy. It plays a minor part in Bordeaux blends and a more important role in the meaty reds of Cahors. But Argentina gets the best out of it, with lushly textured, ripe, damsony reds.

Nebbiolo

This grape is responsible for the fine reds of Barolo and Barbaresco in Italy's Piedmont region. These tannic monsters need a few years to soften out, but you'll be rewarded by the wait—the wines have a wonderful array of aromas and tastes (tar and roses are two classic scents). Outside Italy, Australia is trying hard with the grape and there has been the occasional success in California's Central Coast.

Pinotage

A South African cross between Pinot Noir and the southern French variety Cinsaut, Pinotage hasn't had the best of times. The

worst—and there is still a lot of horrible stuff around—smells like nail polish remover, but in the hands of an experienced winemaker it can produce a serious wine —richly fruity, with plum, redcurrant, and banana flavors.

Sangiovese

Sangiovese sums up Italy. It forms the basis for all Chianti and Brunello di Montalcino, as well as a range of fancy Tuscan and Supertuscan wines (see page 111). It makes wine that has tobacco, cherry-skin aromas and plum fruits with coffee, leather, and even tea thrown in on the finish. It blends well with other varieties such as Cabernet Sauvignon and Merlot, and takes well to new oak. California is also having a go.

Tempranillo

This is Spain's best grape. It is the dominant flavor in Rioja, and appears in many other Spanish wine regions—Ribera del Duero, La Mancha and Valdepeñas to name three—often with its own regional name. Its strawberry, toffee, and spice flavors are delicious when young, but Tempranillo also matures well and marries happily with oak. It has put down roots in California and Oregon and is doing well in Argentina.

Zinfandel

"Zin," as the Californians like to call it, was claimed as their native grape, but it is, in fact, southern Italy's little-known Primitivo grape. The Californians have done great things with it—at best, it makes powerful, supple, ripe cherry, black pepper, plum, and blackberry-flavored reds. It also makes a rather insipid blush wine, and even a late harvest-style dessert wine.

Wines by Style: Whites

"I don't know much about wine, but I know what I like."
How often have you heard this? You've probably said it yourself:
you like dry, crisp whites or meaty reds. Well, here goes.

above Creamy, unoaked Chardonnay and fruity Sauvignon Blanc are refreshing wines with enough body to drink on their own.

Clean and crisp: dry white wines

Fresh, dry-as-a-bone whites are perfect for hot weather or just great with a big bowl of seafood. They are not particularly complex —in fact, when drunk on their own, they can even be a bit of a bore—so consider a splash of crème de cassis for pre-dinner

drinking, or soda water to make a spritzer. As food partners, clean and crisp whites are ideal; their neutral flavors don't fight with ingredients and even aid digestion, cutting through the grease in fattier dishes. Even your Friday night curry isn't out of bounds with clean, crisp whites, as any other wine would be lost in the aromatic spices (but beer is better). And, because the flavors don't exactly pack a punch, you can really chill them down without losing out.

Which are the best?
In France, look to areas such as Entre-deux-Mers, and other simple Bordeaux whites. Or up to the Loire and Muscadet. From Burgundy, there are basic unoaked Chablis and everyday Mâcon Blanc to consider, plus Aligoté. To the east of France there are the Silvaners and Pinot Blancs from Alsace, and in the south, the Côtes du Rhône (though many of these will fall into the next category—the medium white wines).

In Italy, Soave, Verdicchio, Pinot Grigio, Orvieto Secco, and Frascati are all clean, crisp whites, plus Italy's version of Pinot Blanc (Pinot Bianco), and Vermentino, Malvasia, Trebbiano, Lugana and even Chardonnay from the Alto Adige (the Italians like their whites fairly neutral). And don't forget Sicily—she's producing lots of clean, easy drinking, crisp, dry whites. Then there's always Spain. The bulk of

Spanish whites fall into this category—especially good are those from Rueda. Also Portugal and its vinho verde.

Tangy and creamy: medium white wines

These are medium-bodied whites that have a touch of the aromatics, are tangy or creamy, and have a bit more oomph.

Which are the best?

New Zealand Sauvignon Blanc, particularly from Marlborough, is a good tangy choice. In fact, Sauvignon Blanc from most places —South Africa does a particularly pungent version, while Chile's has a softer edge —are pretty much acceptable. The Loire does minerally, even smoky Sauvignon Blanc in Sancerre and Pouilly-Fumé, and there are also the region's sharp-edged Chenin Blancs (give them a bit of age and the honey follows).

Chablis proper falls into the creamy category: the richer, more creamy styles of the best areas, plus other white Burgundy, like a well-made Mâcon-Villages. Chardonnay is, generally, a good creamy, medium white—

as long as it has not been near any oak (once you've got oak, you've got lots of body—see overleaf). Elsewhere in France, consider the tangy whites from the southwest—Jurançon Sec and certain *vins de pays* from the Languedoc.

Most wine-producing countries have medium whites—even England (the tangy Bacchus variety is one to watch). Italy probably produces the least characterful whites of this category, but then Italian whites are made to drink with food—the top stuff from the areas mentioned above will all have a bit more weight so will slip into this medium-bodied section. Spain, too—Rueda's best has more oomph to it—the Verdejo grape used in abundance can be surprisingly tangy. Also look to Somontano and Penedès. Portugal's odd-sounding native varieties also slide onto the medium whites list, as do most white wines from Eastern Europe, Hungary particularly.

Across in North America, Pinot Gris and Chardonnay from west coast areas like

below Match the robust flavors of Provençal cooking with a rich white, such as barrel-aged Sémillon, or drink a gutsy rosé as the locals do.

Oregon fall into the creamy category, as do many whites from Canada. You might think Australia, with its big, blowsy, oaky whites, shouldn't get a look-in here, but have you ever tried a creamy Chardonnay from its cooler climate areas (Tasmania and the Adelaide Hills to name two)?

Rich and succulent: full-bodied white wines

So you like big whites? These wines are rich and succulent, creamy and soft, but they have a dry backbone, like barrel-aged Chardonnay and Sémillon, Marsanne and Roussanne. Oak plays a big part in full-bodied whites.

Which are the best?

Let's start in France with a great white Burgundy from a decent vintage. This is the blueprint for the world's big, lavishly oaked

below The Château Pichon-Longueville-Baronin Pauillac presides over Bordeaux's vineyards, which produce grapes for both white and red wines on their gravel soil.

Chardonnays: from California to New Zealand, Australia, Chile, and South Africa. Australia, though, can take credit for reinventing the Chardonnay grape with its upfront flavors of peach, apricot and mango, a layer of vanilla with butterscotch richness. Even cheaper Australian Chardonnay still manages rich, melon and peach fruits with a layer of sweet oak provided by the more economical toasted wood chips during fermentation.

Elsewhere, Chardonnay takes on a citrus character in Chile, becomes chewier in Argentina and makes blockbusters in California. Italy has done well with Chardonnay—particularly in Tuscany. As has Spain, in Costers del Segre.

Don't fancy Chardonnay? Well, Australia steals a march on other countries with a whole range of full-bodied whites, from Marsanne in the Goulburn Valley to Sémillon in the Hunter Valley—both lush and honeyed, especially if left in the bottle.

Or look to the Graves, in Bordeaux, where they are blending Sémillon and Sauvignon Blanc with certain power—particularly in Pessac-Léognan. There are also the top names in the Rhône to look for, based on Marsanne and Roussanne. Not forgetting white Rioja, based on the Viura grape. And Austria: look at native grape Grüner Veltliner—especially after a few years in the bottle.

Fragrant and fruity: aromatic white wines

Wine's perfume counter—though admittedly not everyone's cup of tea, aromatic white wines are not for knocking back, but they make great aperitifs and memorable matches to certain dishes.

Which are the best?

King of the aromatic grape varieties is Gewürztraminer: think Turkish Delight, dew-covered roses, and fresh lychees. It's made the world over, but it's best in Alsace (where they don't use the *umlaut*, so it's *Gewurztraminer*).

Then there's Riesling. This star grape is still sadly out of fashion (Liebfraumilch hit the nail in Riesling's coffin), but it will be back. Germany still makes the best Riesling, with Alsace following close on its heels. Alsace is also home to a further line-up of other arrestingly aromatic varieties such as Muscat, a fragrant grape if ever there was, and now found in many parts of the wine world. For a less floral alternative, try Australia's efforts with Riesling—they tend to be less heavy on the gas and with more racy lime flavors.

Viognier is another grape that scales astonishing heights on the aromatics scale: its spiritual home is Condrieu, in the northern Rhône, where growers harvest Viognier late, resulting in rich, complex wines with amazing length. California has also managed to produce similarly aromatic fruit with its own version of Viognier, though with lower acidity levels.

You can also look to Spain's northwest corner, where it produces fragrant white wines of great individuality in the form of Albariño from Galicia. Argentina is also making a name for itself with its "native" spicy, musky Torrontés. Hungary produces an array of aromatic dry whites made from varieties such as Irsai Oliver.

Wines by Style: Reds

You like Beaujolais, but you don't like that bottle of Bulgarian red your father-in-law insists on serving with Sunday lunch. No worries—the wine world is still your oyster.

Soft and juicy: light, fruity red wines

Easy gluggers, in other words. Low on tannins, high on fruit and relatively pale in color. Sometimes, you just want to keep things light. These include Gamay, some Pinot Noir, Cabernet Franc from the Loire —from Anjou and Touraine—and Italy's cherry-packed Valpolicellas, Chiarettos, and Bardolinos. Look at reds from predominantly white-wine-producing regions such as the Loire, Germany (the Württemberg), Austria, and Switzerland.

Which are the best?

Beaujolais and the appellations within are the most obvious starting points for light, fruity reds, such as Moulin-à-Vent. It is made from the Gamay grape and it is so light you could almost mistake it for a white wine (and in some cases you can serve them almost as cool). But don't try to age them for more than a few months, because the fruit just falls away completely. Drink them young, either with food or without. The Côtes du Rhône has a fair few soft, juicy reds, too.

Almost any red wine from Italy's Alto Adige will be pretty pale in color, and just across the mountains, you could try Dolcetto from the Piedmont. If you like bubbles, then Lambrusco is the light red for you. Few know about Portugal's red vinho verde, and you should definitely take a look at Spain's vast plains of La Mancha, Navarra, or Valdepeñas.

Pinot Noir from just about anywhere can be classified as soft and juicy, although when its silky, strawberry, mellow fruit achieves heights of greatness, it slips into the medium-bodied, full, and fruity category. The best Pinot Noir is from Burgundy, followed by California—particularly the Carneros region and the Central Coast regions, such as Santa Barbara and Santa Ynez—from Oregon also, and Chile, down south. On the flip side of the globe, Pinot Noir from places such as Martinborough and Marlborough in New Zealand is usually pretty soft and fruity, though some will have enough weight to push them through to the next section.

Full and fruity: medium-bodied red wine

These wines are found in most of Europe. Head south, to the sun, and most reds are huge, full-bodied numbers, although each southern hemisphere country has its own cooler climate wine-growing areas where a medium-bodied red is an achievable feat (such as Pinot Noir).

You can add to this list most of the above soft and fruity reds—when you get the right producer (who has managed to get the best out of his grapes, chosen his vineyard site carefully, and kept a close eye on the weather).

Which are the best?

For medium-bodied reds, don't rule out Bordeaux—just keep to the less serious labels and keep an eye on the vintage (1990 and 1995, for example, were very good vintages, producing pretty powerful fruit—see also page 72). Certain subregions, such as Margaux, will also always tend toward the lighter, more medium-bodied styles.

Most wines made with Merlot sit quite happily in the medium-bodied, full, and fruity red category. This soft, easy fruit is grown the world over, though Californian blockbuster Merlots are happier in the next, huge red category.

far left Young reds and those from mainly white wine producing areas have a delicate fruitiness—perfect for drinking on their own or serving with snacks and al fresco lunches.

below Robust French cooking calls for an accompanying glass—or a bottle—of wine with a bit of oomph and a full, fruity flavor.

Then there's Syrah from the northern Rhône and Grenache from the southern Rhône. The granite soils in the north encourage a big, full, fruity nose, yet acidity levels remain high, lightening up the proceeds considerably. Farther down south, reds from Provence and smaller nearby appellations to the north, south, and west could also wear the medium-bodied hat, though, once again, the best producers push the wines up a notch into the next category.

Italy has a vast line-up of medium-bodied red wines, including those made with Barbera, Nebbiolo, Teroldego, and Sangiovese varieties. Chianti also falls into this category, though better quality, more expensive examples push it up in to the next one. In the north, traditionally full-bodied grapes such as Cabernet Sauvignon rarely achieve more than medium body in Trentino and Friuli. In Spain, look to the younger Riojas—*joven* or *crianza*. In Eastern Europe, most reds never achieve more than medium body, as yields are too high.

Huge reds: full-bodied red wines

The real muscle. A full-bodied red is a meaty, richly flavored mouthful, making other wines look weedy in comparison. Generally, these wines are made in hotter areas, from older vines, and need aging in oak barrels, so tend to be rather more expensive than the rest. In the hands of an expert, in good vintages, many of those in the medium-bodied category can build up enough muscle to be a huge red.

Which are the best?

Cabernet Sauvignon leads the way in the huge reds, a grape that has truly traveled the globe. Its spiritual home, however, is Bordeaux, where as part of a blend it can produce full-bodied reds right across the quality spectrum. The biggest Cabs of all are to be found in California, in the Napa Valley, where they are high in alcohol and big on flavor, with prices to match. The northern Rhône is also home to many robust reds, based on the Syrah grape, as is its Australian namesake, Shiraz, particularly those from the Barossa or McLaren Vale.

If grown in the right soil and climate, many red grapes can pack a serious punch. This includes rich, plummy Californian Zinfandel, earthy Mourvèdre (when grown in Bandol) and Tempranillo, when grown in Spain's top red region of Ribera del Duero or in Rioja (the gran reservas). Spain, in fact, is turning out an ever-increasing selection of meaty reds from newer wine-growing areas such as Toro and Priorato. Portugal, too, has its share of big reds: those from the Douro made with the classic port-grape varieties, and the reds of Bairrada and Dão. And don't rule out Greece; a rising tide of small producers are turning out herbaceous, savory reds.

Leave Europe, and full-bodied reds become the norm, from Argentina to Chile, Australia to South Africa, and back up to California.

In the pink: rosé wines

Rosé is generally not sweet, as the color may suggest. Go to any bar in Pamplona, Spain, and you will see plenty of people swigging pink drinks. The famous bull-running town is in the heart of Navarra, one of Spain's top rosé-producing regions. Made mostly with the Garnacha (Grenache) grape, the wines are a mouthful of strawberries with a zingy acidity: great for washing down salty, hunks of ham—great with many foods in fact.

These are not complex wines, though it is possible to make a serious rosé: a handful of producers have tried it, but generally people won't fork out much for pink wines. Rosé makes a great summer quaffer—it's good with most barbecued food.

Which are the best?

A good place to start looking for pink is in the south of France. Provence is the home of French rosé, and there are many good examples made with grapes such as Mourvèdre and Grenache. Even Bordeaux has been known to lighten up with a few decent pinks; it even has a name for it—*clairet*. Other regions scattered about the country produce reds so pale you might think they were rosé: the Poulsard grape in Jura and Gamay in Beaujolais are just two examples. The Loire makes decent pink too—not the rather sugary Rosé d'Anjou but the altogether more elegant pinks from Sancerre. Outside France and Spain, look at Chile and Argentina for rosé. South Africa and Australia also produce some pink.

Wines by Style: Bubbles

left From a glass of Buck's Fizz on Thanksgiving morning to toasting the new bride and groom, Champagne remains the world's first choice of wine for special occasions.

Which are the best?

The best sparkling wines are made in cool climates and the best area of all is Champagne. East of Paris, it's the most northerly wine-growing region in France. The grapes—Pinot Noir, Chardonnay et al—struggle to ripen fully in the five key growing areas (the best is Montagne de Reims), and are rather tart, to say the least, until transformed by the Champagne method. Why so great? Because the skilled winemakers manage to juggle difficult fruit from different years with the subtle yeast flavors the wine acquires as it lays aging in the chalky cellars.

Each Champagne house has its own style. If you like more flavor in your Champagne, then go for one with more Pinot Noir or Pinot Meunier in the blend —or all black grapes (Blanc de Noirs). If you like them light and creamy, go for a Blanc de Blancs, made from 100 percent Chardonnay.

That's not to say that all Champagne is great—far from it. In fact, the cheapest (the nonvintage) are often wincingly acidic, and the cheaper sweeter styles (demi-sec, doux) can be cloying with their clumsy dosages. The best are those with a vintage date: when the wine has been allowed to age a bit, revealing layers of creamy, buttery, nutty fruit. Watch out for the different vintages—some are richer (like 1990);

Nothing makes you feel more like a party than sparkling wine. And when it's the best stuff —vintage Champagne—nothing lifts the spirits better. Champagne is still the world's number one bubbly, though there are an increasing number of contenders to the throne: producers in Tasmania are attempting a serious coup, as are rebels in nearby New Zealand, plus a handful of renegades in the fog-bound coastal valleys of California. Even England is capable of turning out decent sparklers (when the weather allows).

others are much lighter (like 1992). Don't want to splash out on vintage, or even the better nonvintage? Then consider other regions in France turning out decent bubbly at a fraction of the price, particularly those from the Loire Valley (Crémant de Loire), Burgundy (Crémant de Bourgogne) and Alsace (Crémant d'Alsace). Head farther south, and you'll be rewarded with other interesting sparklers such as Crémant de Die, Gaillac Mousseux and Blanquette de Limoux.

Germany and Austria make okay sparklers called sekt, but really Italy is your next stop for sparkling wine. It makes tons of the stuff. Some of it in the Champagne style, but most of it the low-alcohol, sweet Muscat-based sparklers such as Moscato d'Asti (a step up from the more familiar Asti Spumante), and the red or white Lambrusco. But there's also Prosecco, a speciality of the Veneto that is crisp and refreshing.

Want something softer, not so austere? Look to Catalonia in northern Spain for cava: bags of yeasty, appley fruit—good value, too.

Virtually every wine-producing country makes sparkling wine—technically you can use any grape. The Australians even make sparkling wine from Shiraz, Cabernet Sauvignon, and Grenache (an acquired taste though not bad with the Bar-B-Q), though Australia is much more successful with its Champagne-style blends.

The next two best sparkling-wine-producing countries and regions after Champagne are California and New Zealand. Such a close second, in fact, that Champagne producers have been investing heavily in sparkling wine production in both these countries. The resulting wines are quite different though: peachy, summery fruits for California; more limey, citrus fruit for New Zealand, with the best stuff giving the Champenoise a run for their money.

South Africa is trying hard too, with its Méthode Cap Classique, though results are more variable.

below Regular turning and tapping the bottles, while gradually inverting them, is a laborious but essential task traditionally done by hand. Known as remuage, it is now more often done mechanically.

Wines by Style: Sweet

The best kind of sweet wine is one where the fruit has botrytized, as opposed to getting its sweetness from a sackful of sugar: the grapes are left to ripen fully on the vine, preferably in slightly damp, humid conditions, and then shrivel up and literally rot—or noble rot, as it's called. The resulting wine is highly concentrated and incredibly intense, encouraging elaborate descriptions: luscious, gold-flecked, peach and apricot fruit, laced with honey and nuts.

There are all kinds of sweet wines. Many are delicious—maybe not all stirring the levels of ecstasy described above, but they make happy partners to a whole range of foods—sweet and savory. They range from the delicately scented orange blossom Moscatels from Valencia to gasoliny late harvest Rieslings of Oregon to the syrupy, sweet German and Austrian Beerenauslesen and Trockenbeerenauslesen.

Which are the best?

Top of the sweet wine tree is Sauternes and Barsac, in Bordeaux—the benchmark for the world's sweet winemakers. They are rich, luscious blends of Sémillon and Sauvignon Blanc, with intense flavors of peach, pineapple, preserved lemon, butterscotch, and honey, with a balanced acidity. But they are expensive.

There are cheaper, less concentrated alternatives not a million miles away—from places such as Loupiac and Monbazillac. A little farther to the north, the Loire produces rather unusual sweet wines from Chenin Blanc—try Vouvray. A giant leap east, and Alsace produces a seductive line-up of sweet wines from Vendange Tardive (late harvest) to Séléction de Grains Nobles (selection of botrytis-affected grapes) using an array of grape varieties including Pinot Gris, Gewurztraminer and Riesling. Sweet

though these are (Séléction de Grains Nobles is the sweetest), the high levels of acidity mean they partner some of the region's savory dishes beautifully—the best match is foie gras. Much farther south, and you hit the sweet wines of Jurançon, made from curious-sounding grape varieties such as Gros Manseng. The high-altitude Pyrenean vineyards encourage a zingy acidity, which balances the pineapple and apricot fruit perfectly.

Now Germany. Don't try pronouncing (or drinking) her sweet wines with speed: Trockenbeerenauslese is intensely sweet and the most expensive; Beerenauslese is almost as concentrated; Auslese less so. The best are made from Riesling and the grapes are left on the vine until the last possible moment. It is the same story with neighboring Austria, though the wines are even fatter here. Then there's the Eiswein ("ice wine") made in both countries (and in Canada) from frozen grapes, the sweetest of them all. Pickers harvest these grapes under difficult conditions, the juice is miniscule, and the resulting wine is expensive, but delicious.

Elsewhere, Hungary's Tokaji region turns out stunning sweet wines with an almost sherry-like tang and smoky fruit. Again, botrytis is the key, though the Hungarian tradition is to make an *aszú* (a sweet paste) with all the nobly rotten grapes, which are then fermented with the dry wines to varying levels of sweetness—the number of *puttonyos* of *aszú* (containers of paste) that are added (from three to six) give an indication of the final sweetness.

left Sweet wines vary from the inexpensive, feel-good, delicately fragrant to the luscious, complex, intense, and seriously costly. Both can be drunk on their own or with food.

above Dessert wines rarely taste of grapes; more often, their flavors will be like apricot, peach or pineapple, with a hint of honey, and sometimes even smoky undertones.

Italy has had a long tradition of making sweet wine from semidried or dried grapes. Recioto di Valpolicella is a sweet red packed with plum and cherry fruits; Tuscany's Vin Santo is made with grapes that are dried in attics.

Australia and New Zealand are having a go with botrytis-affected grapes, though the noble rot doesn't develop quite so well in the warmer, drier Antipodean climes, so the wines' sweetness is generally artificially encouraged and therefore won't age so well.

Wines by Style: Fortified

above Sherry, port, and Madeira are the three classic fortified wines, but there are dozens of others in this category.

These include sherry, port, Madeira, Marsala, Rutherglen Muscats, Samos Muscats, the red and whites of Banyuls and Rivesaltes, Greece's pruney Mavrodaphne of Patras—a veritable feast, in other words, ranging in flavor from salty, sourdough (manzanilla sherry) to the liquid Christmas pudding of the Rutherglen Muscats. You'll even find a match for chocolate, and plenty that will go stunningly well with cheese.

Spain and Portugal

Fino and manzanilla: these two sherry styles from Jerez in Spain are the driest of the world's fortified wines. They are very pale in color and lean in fruit, but have a salty, yeasty, mineral flavor that partners many foods perfectly. The Spanish drink it as you would a bottle of wine. Both styles make a fine aperitif.

An aged fino is called amontillado, which also makes a great aperitif, as do the other drier sherry styles of palo cortado and oloroso, both with a delicious nuttiness and higher acidity levels. Add some sugar and you've got cream sherry. This tends to swamp the delicate fruit flavors. It's not to be confused with oloroso dulce, a delicious, rare sherry with beautifully concentrated fruit. The most intense sherry of all is PX— Pedro Ximénez—made from sun-dried grapes. It's licorice black and very raisiny.

Another of the world's great fortified wines, port, is from Portugal. Others have tried to imitate (in South Africa and Australia) but no one comes near. Port grapes (among them Touriga Nacional, Tinta Barroca, and Tinta Roriz) are grown on vertiginous terraces along the banks of the Douro in northern Portugal. Port styles range from the basic ruby and the rather coarse white ports, to cask-aged tawnies and single quinta ports, to the finest vintage ports, aged for 20 years or more.

Madeira also excites, with an intriguing range of aromas and flavors. The sub-tropical island produces the world's most oxidized wine. It is heated in huge vats (hence the word "maderized")—the cheap stuff artificially, the best stuff in sun-drenched attics. The main grapes used are Malmsey, Boal, Verdelho, and Sercial. The wine is then aged naturally in all that sub-tropical warmth. The resulting wines range from dry, nutty Sercial to fruitcake Malmsey.

France and Italy

France produces a certain amount of forti-fied wines, too, from the honeyed Pineau des Charentes to the red and white fortified wines of Banyuls and Rivesaltes. Banyuls is one of the few wines that go with chocolate, and many a French chef has created savory dishes that go well with it too. And not to forget its neighbor, the port-like Maury, one

of Roussillon's most famous vins doux naturels, which like Banyuls is made predominantly from Grenache Noir.

Italy has Marsala. It is a beloved ingredient in the kitchen as well as on the table after dinner. The cheap stuff is rather confected, but the best dry Marsala is smooth, nutty, and buttery.

Other countries

The two southern hemisphere countries that have gone for fortified wines in a big way are Australia and South Africa. Both produce decent port-style wines, and even a sort of sherry (though sales of these have died away in recent years). Australia's Rutherglen region has had particular success with its fortified Liqueur Muscats. The chocolate covered caramel flavors make a fabulous partner for blue cheese.

below Madeira vintages are not declared until the wine is a minimum of 20 years old. Even then, it is best kept several years more.

pour
and enjoy

You're off to a picnic, a barbecue, a smart dinner party; you've got

the girls round for dinner and a video; you're having Friday night in

with a spicy pizza; you've got to organize the wine for the office

party; you're impressing a new girlfriend; you've got a vegan coming

round for lunch... read on, there's a wine for every occasion. There

are rules, too, for matching food and wine, or rather no rules: red

wine and fish—go for it; wine and chocolate—there are partners

out there. Some ingredients always prove tricky, it's just that a little

more thought is required. Same goes for serving temperatures—too

warm and the wine tastes jammy; too cold and you miss out on the

fruit, and that word of warning is aimed at restaurants, too—turn

the tables by making sure you get the best out of your waiter.

Wines for Different Occasions

Apart from opening up a whole new world of wine for yourself, choosing the right wine for the right occasion can make the difference between a good time and a great time.

above Holidaytime is a time to splash out on a selection of wines planned as carefully as you plan the menu.

Christmas and Thanksgiving

It is a time for overindulgence, so let's see if we can lighten the load: smoked salmon is often on the festive menu, and a good, rather unusual match is Bacchus from England. Its elderflower and lime fruits go particularly well with the ubiquitous dill sauce. For the bird itself, try a peachy Viognier from the Pays d'Oc, or a gamey Pinot Noir from Burgundy. With rich dessert, a sweet oloroso is just the thing. In fact, you could forgo a rich fruit pudding altogether and just drink it in liquid form: a Pedro Ximénez from Jerez (or PX, to its mates) or an Australian Liqueur Muscat. And if they are too big too handle, try a Banyuls from the south of France.

New Year's

Bubbles, bubbles, and more bubbles. Start with the good stuff. Champagne from a good producer and a great vintage. Don't save the best until last—at midnight you may have had too much already to notice. A real hedonist could keep this up all night, choosing a Blanc de Noirs for the meatier courses, through to a demi-sec with dessert. Or you could go for a classy sparkling number from the New World: from Tasmania, New Zealand, or California.

Halloween

Or any cold winter's night. Big, meaty, earthy, truffley reds to go with big, meaty, truffley stews: reds from Bandol and Bairrada, Amarone, Eastern European Cabernets and New World Syrahs. With tagines, a great winter staple, try something native—an aromatic, spice-laden red from Morocco or the Lebanon, or a pruney Primitivo from southern Italy, or any of Italy's unusual but spicy southern varieties. For winter sipping predinner, turn to the richer styles of sherry, such as a nutty, but dry oloroso.

above A bottle of Dolcetto makes a fine accompaniment to roasted vegetables.

Outdoor eating: picnic

It is important to think about the weather: avoid heavily oaked Chardonnay and jammy Shiraz in hot weather. Go for a good all-rounder, something that goes equally well with meat as it does with a bowl of strawberries, such as Navarra rosé, or in fact any rosé. It's positively steamy? You want something super-cold and pretty neutral—quenching your thirst is the name of the game: Pinot Grigio would fit the bill, so would Portugal's Vinho Verdes.

below Serve a glass or two of wine while you barbecue the meat and fish.

Outdoor eating: barbecue

This sort of depends how good you are at making barbecues. Add the meat or fish on the grill when the flames are still jumping, and you're talking toast—most wine will be lost in all that bitterness. Wait until the coals turn white before cooking and you'll get sweet, sticky, succulent, charbroiled flavors: for beef, choose Shiraz; for lamb, an inky Zinfandel or a gutsy Ribera del Duero; for swordfish, try a vanilla-laced Chilean Chardonnay; with roasted vegetables, try a Dolcetto.

Midsummer's night

Summertime, and the livin' is easy: floral, aromatic Argentinean Torrontés; less costly Burgundy-style Aligoté; an Australian Riesling—all freshly squeezed limes and grapefruits. Rueda, in Spain, is turning out some very fresh, citrus whites, so is Ribeiro —both would go down well on a warm summer's night. As would a Muscadet— *sur lie* is best. And, if you can find it, try Albariño—Spain's top white from its verdant northwest corner. You want a nice summer red? Consider a lightly chilled Beaujolais (preferably a Cru).

Anniversaries

Year one, serve Champagne—but vintage —you're still on a high. Years two to nine there's still good cause for celebration, so more bubbles, though a supermarket non-vintage will do just fine. Year ten, crack open nonvintage from a good producer —you've defied statistics. Year 20 and you've seen it all before, so something more mellow—an old bottle of Burgundy or Rioja, or an old Riesling from Alsace. Year 50 and, well, it's half a century —congratulate yourselves—it's back to the vintage, and make it a good one.

Birthdays

Find out their favorite wine and choose one from a good producer (your wine store will help you). For the ultimate extravagance, find a wine from their birth year. If old Bordeaux or Burgundy is out of reach, then look to the north of Portugal and a vintage port.

For 18th and 21st birthdays—well, fine wine isn't exactly high on the list for the young palate, so putting beer to one side for the moment, there are plenty of suitable, easy-glugging, fruit-driven New World wines around, from Merlot to Chardonnay.

Weddings

Champagne is probably the most obvious choice. But as we may be talking up to (or over) a hundred drinkers, your most economical bet is a good supermarket nonvintage. And don't get hung up on the name; there are plenty of good sparkling wines from all over the world that would happily fit the bill: the best from the New World include a zesty, yeasty sparkler from Marlborough, New Zealand; an appley, nutty fizz from Tasmania; a smart, savory bubbly from Sonoma. Cheaper bubblies include northern Italian fizz Moscato d'Asti or Prosecco plus the Crémants from France. You could do as the Spanish do, and serve fino or manzanilla, or even think pink.

BEFORE A MEAL

Sherry is a much misunderstood drink and it has been sadly brushed aside in recent years. Cream sherry can take much of the blame. This sweetened sherry style, a favorite of aged aunts, is not drunk in its home country —oh, no, they drink it dry. Fino, manzanilla and the drier styles of amontillado and oloroso make fabulous predinner drinking. There's also kir—of course, a slug of crème de cassis can jazz up a neutral white a treat. Champagne gets the gastric juices going like nothing else, as do the lighter styles of wine from Alsace.

AFTER A MEAL

Two words are important here: sweet wine. These invariably taste much better on their own or with something savory, such as cheese, than they do with most desserts. Many sweet wines can be delicious after a meal, and those with a good kick of acidity (from Germany, Austria, the Loire, or Jurançon) can even refresh the palate. This is also the time to serve the sweeter fortified wines: port, sherry, Madeira, Australian Liqueur Muscats, Banyuls, and the southern French sweet Muscats.

The dinner party

If you know that the wine you are bringing is to be consumed that night, be a good guest and phone ahead. Find out what is on the menu and match it up accordingly (a shellfish supper and a tannic bottle of red is not the best of pairings). You forgot? Well, the wine world's your oyster. Go for something away from the mainstream—a big Barolo from Piedmont, or a nice spicy number from the northern Rhône, or one of Chile's top, plummy Merlots, or a silky Pinot Noir from California. A half-bottle of something sweet will also bring a smile: a good Sauternes or Monbazillac, or a late harvest Riesling.

Cosy dinner for two

Bubbles to start (vintage, of course) followed by mature Burgundy, then a glass of ice wine (from Germany, Austria, or Canada) in place of dessert—but that's the fantasy list. The sensible and more economical option would be to split a half bottle of manzanilla

left Of course, you want the best on your wedding day, but better a good sparkling wine than an indifferent Champagne.

between you while you nibble on salted almonds and marinated olives, followed by a decent Chablis, while you munch on broiled lobster, with a warming brandy to finish. For smooth and approachable, choose Spain; for something that has a bit more bite, go with Cognac or Armagnac.

Vegetarian or vegan

No worries. There are plenty of wines around now that measure up. Didn't know that wine wasn't already vegetarian? Well, you haven't got to the last chapter yet. Animal products are used during fining (the process of removing solid particles from the finished wine): egg whites, casein (milk protein), isinglass (fish bladder), ox blood and gelatin. A growing number of

below Vegetarians needn't miss out, as there is an increasing number of wines produced without using animal products.

producers, vegetarians will be pleased to know, are using alternative fining agents. Your local store should be able to point you in the right direction.

The takeaway

Fried chicken: Californian sparkling wine, would you believe, makes an ideal match. The searing acidity cuts through any grease and the coating won't overwhelm the wine's yeasty, nutty flavors. Failing that, a clean, dry Pinot Blanc from Alsace or one of Italy's neutral, but refreshing whites.

Pizza: It's got to be Chianti, or one of California's Italian numbers. A medium-bodied Chardonnay—not too heavy on the oak—works well too.

Chinese: Alsace is your girl for this (Gewurztraminer, especially)—or German Riesling. Prefer a red? Then choose something light—a Beaujolais, perhaps.

Finally, curry: Beer is best, but if you

above For something livelier than jasmine tea with a stir-fry, try an aromatic German wine.

insist, then choose something aromatic, like a Muscat or a crisp Jurançon made with Gros Manseng, or a Marsanne, for a bit more weight.

A night in alone

Who said drinking alone was sad? Okay, well maybe not every night, upon night, upon night—but in moderation, when there's a good film on TV—what could be nicer? And you don't have to drink the whole bottle either—that's what wine preservation systems are for, such as Wine Saver, and VacuVin. Curling up in front of a fire with bottle of soft, fruity, juicy New World Merlot is just the thing. So is a ripe, tangy Aussie Verdelho and a plate piled high with roasted vegetables; or a bowl of spaghetti carbonara and a bottle of Orvieto.

left Add a touch of romance to a mundane takeaway supper with a glass of wine.

Australia, or a fruity Grüner Veltliner from Austria. For reds, go light, a Bardolino from the Veneto is one option, or something from the great plains of Spain.

A night in with your buddies

There's no point in presenting anything too serious, you've got more important things to talk about—but you want to impress just a smidgen nonetheless. To kick off, a young Marsanne or a limey South African Chenin Blanc. A Sauvignon-Sémillon works well on its own too. Then with the spaghetti and meat sauce, try Dolcetto, or a black pepper and plum spice Zinfandel.

Office party

Begin with bubbles, they break the ice. For winter, a brut, which is clean, dry, and not too acidic. Cava is good value, though avoid the cheapest, which are a tad hot on the finish. Bubbles aside, you want something dry, but racy, and not too oaky, nor too acidic. You could try a Riesling from

"Bring a bottle" parties

A wine, in other words, that can be drunk all night long: no eye-watering acidity, nor too much wood, or too much alcohol. Alsace, again, you've got lots of choice here. You could choose a less aromatic Sauvignon Blanc (those from Bordeaux, for example) or a Chardonnay—unoaked—from Languedoc or southern hemisphere countries. An Italian Pinot Grigio, for example, is a good bet. You might want to avoid the risk of ruining your carpet by not offering your guests red, though you could opt for a lighter style, such as a slightly chilled Moulin-à-Vent (from France's Beaujolais region).

below For a girls' night in, chill a couple of fragrant and fruity bottles, kick off your shoes and let down your hair.

Food and Wine Pairing: the Basics

above Red wine and broiled salmon work: try Pinot Noir instead of your ususal white wine.

Things have moved on from the white with fish, red with meat days. Food has changed, wines have changed. That's not to say anything goes—it doesn't. A bad clash can spoil a meal completely: try drinking a dry wine with sweet food and the wine will taste thin and acidic; or try eating a delicate piece of steamed fish with a hugely tannic red—it won't work. And there's no point whatsoever splashing out on a mature Burgundy if you are going to team it up with something really hot and spicy.

The first basic rule to follow is to balance the weight of the food with the weight of the wine. There's no point, for example, in putting a light Grenache with a rich venison stew; it simply wouldn't stand up. But put it with a red Bandol, and the match is made. The bolder the flavor of the dish, the bolder the wine must be to stand up to it.

If you are planning to serve more than one wine in a meal, serve lighter wines before full-bodied wines, and drier wines before sweeter wines.

Take into account the sauce that is served with a dish, and the way something is cooked—steaming a piece of fish results in a far more delicate flavor than the sweet, caramelized flavors that are produced when it is broiled.

Here are a few more things you need to consider before settling down with your chosen bottle and plate of food.

Acidity

An acidic wine will cut through fat like a dream, making a dish seem less rich. An acidic wine can also heighten the flavor of a dish—just as a squeeze of lemon might do. And talking of lemons, or vinegar, or any other dish packed with citrus fruits—the accompanying wine must have equal acidity or it will taste flat. This generally means white wine here, but there are a few high acid reds to choose from. You could also choose a red with low tannins, because

above Meat goes well with chewy, tannic wine—it smoothes out the tannins a treat.

tannin clashes with acidic food—try Pinot Noir or Beaujolais. Some rosés will also work in this situation.

Sweetness

A general rule of thumb is that the wine must be at least as sweet as the food—and can be even sweeter. If you get it the wrong way around, the wine will taste tart and thin. Pairing sweet and savory is more of a challenge. There are famous marriages, such as Sauternes and foie gras, Stilton and port; and not so famous pairings that are just as good, such as scallops in a creamy sauce with German Spätlese.

Tannin

There's only one true partner for a chewy, tannic wine—meat. It smoothes out the tannins perfectly. There are many fine gutsy Italians (such as Nebbiolo and Brunello) that are let down badly without a plate of meat. But cheese trips up horribly around tannin, as do eggs. Fish and tannic reds? Not likely!

right Muscadet is great with seafood.

The Perfect Partner

Nibbles

The perfect partner for olives, salted almonds and cheesey bits is manzanilla or fino. These bone dry, tangy sherries are hugely fashionable in their home country, Spain, but have taken a while to get going elsewhere. But try them—you'll be pleasantly surprised. To get the gastric juices going for the following meal, a little acidity is called for. Champagne, of course, starts things off with great style, as do bubbles from California or New Zealand.

Fish

Fish needs white wine. Wrong. And that's too general. What sort of white? What sort of fish is it? Flounder and swordfish are poles apart in terms of flavor. Are you going to grill it, steam it, poach it, or fry it? Are you going to serve a sauce with it—a vinegary caper butter for skate wing, for exam-

ple? Broil a piece of wild salmon and a wooded white will do the trick far better than a neutral Orvieto. Apply that weight rule: match the weight of the food with the weight of the wine. Clean, fresh seafood needs clean, tangy wines: you could even choose manzanilla sherry, with its salty tang. And what about fish and red wine? Pan-fried tuna goes down extremely well with an Oregon Pinot Noir; even salmon and Merlot works.

Meat

Like fish, it depends how you cook it. Roast a leg of lamb with just rosemary for embellishment and the wine world's your oyster: Rioja, Ribera del Duero, Bordeaux, Burgundy—almost any red with a bit of weight. But smother your meat in Moroccan spices and whack it in a tagine and you've got to start thinking. There's

some chili and a plethora of aromatics, so go light on the tannins and up-front with the fruit—a Grenache from the south of France, say, or even a Zinfandel from California's Central Coast. For anything gamey, think earthy, gamey flavors in wine: Pinot Noir, Bandol, Nebbiolo.

Vegetables

Vegetables need tangy whites, such as Australian Riesling or New Zealand Sauvignon Blanc. Again, think about how you are going to cook your vegetables. If you are roasting them, go for something more intensely flavored and aromatic with a good acidity: Alsace Riesling, or a young Australian Verdelho or Pinot Gris from Oregon. If your vegetables are served on the side, the protein will take center stage. With a big bowl of salad tossed in a zippy dressing, a zippy, zesty wine is best: a crisp Muscadet sur lie, a Soave or a Pinot Grigio.

Desserts

There are only really two things to remember. The first is to drink a wine that is at least as sweet—if not sweeter—than what you are eating. Why? Because you'll lose the flavor of the wine in the sweetness

left If your fish is simply broiled, try a clean, sharp white.

right Salads need a crisp, lively wine, but be careful not to clash with the dressing.

of the dessert. Second, forget matching up wine with anything frozen—ice cream and wine just don't mix: though there is one exception—a drizzle of PX (Pedro Ximénez sherry) over vanilla ice cream is delicious. You could also try and match up the particular flavors of your chosen dessert with a particular style of wine, say an apricot and almond tart with an apricoty, roasted nutty Passito di Pantelleria from southern Italy.

Cheese

This is one myth that needs blowing out of the water: red wine and cheese go together. They don't, mostly. White wine is generally a far better match. And the stronger the cheese, the sweeter the wine. Ever tried a sweeter style of sherry with Stilton? Or Sauternes with Roquefort? Both are marvelous matches. Australian Liqueur Muscats are great with blue, too. Goat's cheese loses its way completely with a tannic red—it's far better with a Loire Valley Sauvignon Blanc. Ripe Camembert-types need wine with a bit more oomph—some oak, even.

Tricky Ingredients

Some ingredients give you a hard time when choosing a wine to match—but don't panic, there's a match for virtually everything, though in some cases you may have to search for it.

Vinegar

The alarm bells ring loudest with vinegar. It's a real no-go for most wine and that goes for pickled vegetables, too. Try using a more mellow, less acid vinegar such as sherry or balsamic—or even a splash of wine in your dressing. Make sure you rinse capers thoroughly before adding to sauces and avoid the combination of chutney and wine.

Smoked foods

Depends on the level of smokiness. You can forget kippers and wine—try an Islay malt whisky instead. Smoked mackerel makes any wine taste metallic. Smoked salmon is more forgiving: an old Grüner Veltliner from Austria makes a fabulous match, as are lightly oaked New World Chardonnays and the more aromatic Alsace varieties. Champagne cuts through the oily fish, especially a brut with more Chardonnay in the blend. Smoked meats aren't so tricky; just remember to balance up the gutsy flavors with a gutsy wine.

Yogurt

Yogurt is simply not good with wine. The Greeks have got it right serving up their resinated whites (retsina) with yogurt-based dishes such as tzatziki—it really is the only possible pairing.

above Tomatoes are very acid, so choose a low acid red wine, such as Dolcetto, which also has a hint of spice.

Eggs

On their own, eggs are rather tricky when it comes to wine. Give the egg a punchy sauce and a different set of rules applies: just concentrate on matching the wine with the sauce. White wines tend to be better than red with eggy dishes. Lightly oaked Chardonnay copes well with egg-based sauces such as hollandaise, and goes well with quiches, because of the pastry.

Chocolate

Contrary to popular opinion, there are matches for chocolate. For the dark, bitter, high content cocoa kind, go for Maury. Tawny port and rich chocolate desserts are a fabulous combination. And if you dare, Australian Liqueur Muscat.

Chili

Tannin and chili do not mix. If it's a red you're after, go for softer, lighter grape varieties such as Gamay or New World Pinot Noirs. New World Merlot is great with Tex-Mex food. For whites, stay cool and neutral; any finesse will be lost.

Ginger

Ginger isn't as bad with wine as you would think but it needs something aromatic to stand up to it: Argentina's Torrontés copes well, as do Riesling and Gewurztraminer from Alsace and elsewhere. The Muscat family doesn't do badly either, and Viognier deserves a look-in.

Citrus fruits

The wine must match the acidity of the citrus dish, whether sweet or savory. For grapefruit flavors try a Gros Manseng from the Jurançon, or for lemon, an Australian Verdelho or a Clare Valley Riesling. For lemony desserts, try a late harvest Riesling. For orangey desserts a marmaladey Setúbal from Portugal works well. For duck and orange, stay in Germany.

Tomato

Tomatoes are very high in acidity. For a rich, tomato sauce on spaghetti, a northern Italian, such as Dolcetto, works well. With freshly sliced tomatoes, go for Sauvignon Blanc or Pinot Grigio.

Artichokes

A famously bad partner for wine—but Portugal's underrated Dão region has white wines that stand up. New Zealand's Sauvignon Blanc also makes the match.

right A wine with an intense flavor, such as Australian Sémillon, can stand up well to an orange sauce.

TRICKY INGREDIENTS

Vinegar	German Riesling Kabinett
Smoked foods	for salmon try Austrian Grüner Veltliner, German or Alsace Riesling, Blanc de Blancs Champagne; for meat try Pinot Noir, Nebbiolo or Zinfandel
Yogurt	Retsina, Italian dry whites, rosé
Eggs	Cheaper white Burgundy, Alsace Pinot Blanc, Pinot Grigio
Chocolate	for lighter chocolate desserts try cheap Muscats or Recioto; for richer chocolate desserts try Maury, tawny port, Australian Liqueur Muscats
Chili	New World Sauvignon Blanc, Beaujolais, New World Pinot Noirs and Merlot, Shiraz
Ginger	Torrontés, Riesling, Alsace Gewurztraminer, Dry Muscats, Viognier, Sauvignon Blanc
Citrus fruits	for grapefruit try Gros Manseng; for savory lemon, Sauvignon Blanc; for sweet lemon try late harvest Riesling; for savory orange, Australian Sémillon or German Riesling; for sweet orange try Setúbal
Tomato	for sauce try Dolcetto or Sangiovese; for salads try Sauvignon Blanc or Pinot Grigio
Truffles	Red Bandol, Old Burgundy, Rioja, Douro Reds
Artichokes	Dão whites, New Zealand Sauvignon Blanc, Verdicchio
Asparagus	Sauvignon Blanc, unoaked Chardonnay, Pinot Blanc

Cooking with Wine

above As with any ingredient, the better the wine you cook with —within reason—the finer the finished dish.

Can I use a wine that's been open for a while in my stew? Can I use a corked wine for cooking? Can I use this eye-wateringly acidic white for my ossobuco? Will I get tipsy from eating moules marinière? No, is the answer to all of these questions.

Add an oxidized wine to your stew and it will taste like you've cooked it in vinegar. If you have a little wine left over after dinner, freeze it in resealable plastic bags for adding to sauces, or using for marinades (it works).

Add a splash of corked wine to a sauce and it will concentrate the mustiness further. While it is not worth using your best bottle in a four-hour braised lamb dish (the wine will forever be entwined with the

meat juices), the basic characteristics of a wine will be passed on to the finished dish —so don't use your cheapest bottle either.

A general rule of thumb is that if it's good enough to drink, it's good enough to cook with. Red wines give a greater depth of flavor than white wines. But the more acidic the wine, the more acidic the sauce will be, so avoid cooking with tart white wines, and cut whites with equal amounts of water for cooking.

Cooking with wine is common in many countries. It adds a depth and dimension to a dish in a way that no other ingredient can. Wine can mellow to a remarkable richness when it is simmered in sauces, braises, or stews. Once alcohol hits the heat, it becomes progressively less alcoholic (it also boils quicker than water). It can transform the humblest cut of meat and perk up a none-too-fresh piece of angler fish. Wine can be used at every stage of cooking, from tenderizing meat to baking pears.

Stocks

Wine is often used instead of, or often as well as, water as a base for soups and sauces. Wine features in many risotto dishes and while red wine is used in game stock, white wine is added to chicken and fish stocks.

Marinating

There's a rich aromatic Greek winter dish of meat (beef, pork, rabbit, or hare) first marinated overnight in red wine, then baked slowly for five hours until the meat is tender. Fabulous. It just shows what can be achieved with a little forward planning, a bottle of red and a cheap cut of meat. Marinate meat with red or white wine, then use the marinade for deglazing, or as a base for a sauce. For quick marinades, try using Madeira or sherry.

Deglazing

Add a slug of wine to the frying pan or roasting tin after you've taken the meat out and it will lift off the sticky bits crusted on to the bottom. Let it reduce, strain it, and you've got a great sauce.

Court-bouillon

A court-bouillon is a stock with a slug of wine added (the fruitier, the better), which is used mainly for poaching fish and shellfish, but also for preparing variety meats and white meats. It does wonders for a whole salmon. Generally, red or white can be used, though it's best to stick to white for shellfish.

Sauces

There are many classic sauces that use wine —most of them French. Chateaubriand is frequently served with Beárnaise sauce and potatoes—the sauce is made with white wine and shallots, finished with butter, chopped tarragon, a few drops of lemon juice and a pinch of cayenne; Bercy is a sauce containing fish stock, shallots, fish velouté, butter and parsley; Périgueux is a Madeira sauce with diced truffles.

Stews

Coq au vin is the classic wine stew and there are plenty more. The combination of meat (or fish) and slow cooking with a bottle of wine always produces something rich and tasty. Each wine-producing country has its own wine-based stews, which are best washed down with the same wine you've cooked with.

Desserts

Ever poached pears in red wine? No? Well, you should. For such a simple procedure, the results are dramatic and always impress. Or how about macerating strawberries in a little red wine? It brings out the flavor a treat. There are many recipes where wine is used in desserts – from Marsala in the Italian trattoria staple zabaglione to the British sherry-soaked trifle.

below As in many wine-producing countries, cooking with wine is a way of life in Italy.

Classic Wine Dishes

Many recipes from all over the world use wine to enhance the flavor of a dish. Here are three of the classics. Others include risotto con vongole; daube of beef; coq au vin; Sauerbraten; octopus in red wine; stifado; trifle and zabaglione.

MOULES MARINIÈRES (serves eight)

INGREDIENTS

7 pints/4 litres live mussels
scant ½ cup/100 ml white wine
1 onion, roughly chopped
4 shallots, roughly chopped

freshly ground black pepper
10 tbsp/150 g/1¼ sticks butter
1 tbsp parsley, chopped

METHOD

1 Clean the mussels by scrubbing the shells and removing any beards.
  Throw away any mussels with broken shells or any that don't close when tapped.
2 Put the mussels in a large pan with the wine, onion, shallots, pepper, and butter
  and sauté them over a high heat for 3–4 minutes until the mussels have opened.
  Discard any that do not open.
3 Sprinkle the mussels with parsley.
4 Serve with Muscadet sur lie or a crisp Italian such as an Orvieto, or Verdicchio.

DAUBE D'AUBERGINES (serves six)

INGREDIENTS

1 lb 10 oz/750 g eggplant	2–3 tsp sugar
salt	1 garlic clove, crushed
1 lb 10 oz/750 g tomatoes,	1 tsp dried thyme
peeled and chopped	1 bay leaf
2 tbsp/30 ml red wine	olive oil
freshly ground black pepper	bunch of parsley, finely chopped

METHOD

1 Peel eggplant, cut in half lengthways and then into thick slices.

2 Sprinkle with salt and leave to drain in a colander for half an hour.

3 Meanwhile, put tomatoes, wine, salt, pepper, sugar, garlic, thyme, and bay leaf
in a large pot and simmer over a gentle heat for about 20 minutes.

4 Rinse salt off the eggplant slices, dry them, then shallow-fry in oil until browned.
Soak up excess oil by draining on paper towels.

5 Add the eggplant to the tomato sauce and simmer gently, adding water
if necessary, for about half an hour.

6 Add parsley toward the end of cooking.

7 Serve with gutsy red Vin de Pays.

BOEUF BOURGUIGNONNE (serves eight)

INGREDIENTS

4 lb 8 oz/2 kg stewing steak,	1 tbsp tomato paste
chopped in large chunks	40 button onions, peeled
10 tbsp/150 g pork fat	9 oz/250 g bacon, cut into small strips
⅔ cups/75 g all-purpose flour	¼ cup/50 g butter
2 garlic cloves, crushed	1 tbsp parsley, chopped
2 bottles red Burgundy	salt and pepper

METHOD

1 In a pan brown the beef in the fat over a medium heat.

2 Add the flour and the garlic and season to taste.

3 Pour in the wine and a little water.

4 Stir in the tomato paste.

5 In a separate pan lightly brown the onions and bacon in the butter, then add to the beef.

6 Cook, covered for 3–3½ hours at 275°F/140°C/Gas Mark 1.

7 Sprinkle with parsley and serve with—what else but red Burgundy?

Serving Wine

Make mine a large one

Don't spoil your latest wine discovery by pouring it into a mean-sized glass. You want to be able to appreciate all those lovely aromas in a decent-sized glass. When you take a sip—believe it or not—the shape of your glass makes a difference to the taste of the wine: the particular curvature of a glass determines where the wine lands in your mouth, affecting your taste buds accordingly.

An Austrian glass manufacturer, called Georg Riedel, has built up a worldwide reputation on the theory that the shape of the glass affects the aroma as well as the taste of a wine. He has come up with hundreds of different shaped wine glasses,

above Although glasses with tulip-shaped bowls are the best choice for both red and white, those for red wines should be larger.

each corresponding to the particular flavor components of a grape variety. Not only that, but there are wine glasses shaped for a particular grape variety from a certain region—so a more gooseberry Sauvignon Blanc from New Zealand, for example, gets a different shaped glass to a more grassy Sauvignon Blanc from Sancerre, in France. And the age of the wine, too, makes a difference to the shape: Riedel has designed one glass for nonvintage Champagne and another for vintage Champagne, to appreciate fully the wines' different aromas. This is still pretty revolutionary stuff and unless you are a real wine buff, you probably won't want to take things quite so far.

At the most basic level, however, you should have two types of wine glasses, ideally both with tulip-shaped bowls and long, slender stems. Think big for reds and not quite so big for whites. In fact, as far as reds are concerned, the bigger the glass, the better. Reds, particularly mature reds, need a bit more space to breathe, so you can release those gorgeous, fruity aromas. Remember not to fill the glass to the top, about halfway is best.

If you are a regular sparkling wine drinker, then you'll need flutes. There's a good reason for the tall, thin shape—it keeps in the bubbles (or mousse, to use the correct terminology). Forget those wide-mouthed versions (originally modeled, as legend would have it, on Marie Antoinette's breasts), the wine goes flat in an instant.

Sherry, or any of the fortified wines come to that, needs something slightly smaller than a normal wine glass because of their higher alcoholic strengths. You could follow Spain's example with a copita, the traditional glass of the sherry region, which would do for the other fortified wines too. But never, never use those tiny liqueur glasses still used (sadly) by a large number of bars and restaurants.

Avoid unsightly rims, too. The chunky rim of the ubiquitous 6 oz Paris goblet, for example, detracts from the overall enjoyment of the wine. These clumsily machine-made wine glasses, with their mean measures, have restricted our enjoyment of wine and should be binned immediately. There are plenty of good examples of economical, rim-free, machine-made

wine glasses available in the malls. Also try to use crystal. There are many economical options available from Eastern Europe. But avoid cut crystal—it might look pretty but you can't appreciate the color of the wine properly. The same goes for colored stemware—it distorts the appearance of the wine.

A final word on storage and cleaning. It's not a good idea to store your wine glasses upside down as it traps the stale air and will even taint a delicate wine. Nor should you store glasses in a smoky atmosphere. Even the slightest trace of detergent can affect the taste of wine, so just use hot water. Avoid grease—it'll flatten bubbles in a jiffy. Keep a lint-free cloth just for drying glasses.

below As they are stronger, fortified wines, such as sherry, are served in slightly smaller glasses (top), while Champagne is served in flutes (bottom) to keep the bubbles in.

Corks and Corkscrews

One day all bottles of wine may have a screw top—sounds outrageous, I know. Imagine the drama of dusting off a bottle of top Bordeaux only to unceremoniously unscrew it at the table. In fact, Bordeaux and other fine wine producers the world over will probably fight such a move to their death. But so far, research has shown that only snobbery is preventing the widespread use of screw tops.

A handful of the world's top producers have gone down the plastic cork route, but most wines with plastic corks are still at the cheaper end of the market.

And what of wine-boxes? They are a perfectly good idea, in fact, and there is no reason why more expensive wine shouldn't be sold this way. Likewise cartons, but they are rather tricky to open and choice is limited. Wine in a can? Forget it, bad idea.

But why find an alternative to cork in the first place? After all, it plays a part in the mysterious aging process of wine.

The answer is that corks are prone to infection and shrinkage, which can affect the wine in varying degrees—from a smell and taste that ranges from a touch of the vinegars to full-out dank cellar. Most of us might not even recognize a wine with cork taint, but just ditch it because it doesn't taste very good. If you learn to recognize the smell, then you can do something about it: return the wine to the store you bought it from and get a replacement.

below Traditional corks may eventually be replaced with more modern methods.

left The Screwpull and the "waiter's friend" are among the most popular of the many corkscrew designs.

Of them all, I'd go for the Screwpull. It's an American invention that has since been copied around the globe. Plus, there's a long-handled version for extra leverage. Second choice would be the "waiter's friend"—it is, indeed, still the essential tool of the wine waiter the world over, and it folds away neatly.

Now to work

Cut the foil around the top of the bottle. You can buy a device called a foil cutter that will do the job cleanly and swiftly. Wipe away any dirt from the lip. Press the point of the corkscrew gently into the center of the cork and turn slowly until the point emerges at the bottom of the cork. Then ease out gently.

For sparkling wine, after tearing off the foil and the wire cage, place one hand on the bottle and the other on the cork. Turn the bottle slowly while twisting the cork in the other direction, remembering to point away from people.

below After cutting around the foil and wiping off any dirt around the rim, insert the point of the corkscrew. Ease out the cork gently and smoothly.

How does the cork become damaged?

There's not really any conclusive evidence yet, but the finger of blame is currently pointing at the cork processing itself: corks (many from Portugal and Spain's cork oak forests) are normally bleached in chlorine before washing and drying, which can inadvertently produce something called chloroanisoles, some of which, for instance 2,4,6-trichloranisole (or TCA), can be smelt even in tiny quantities. The cork industry is trying its best to address these problems by replacing the chlorine bleaching with other processes. But this isn't the only culprit – corks are exposed to other evils—such as bad storage practices and even bad smells in container ships.

Removing the cork

Enough of the science. Let's get the cork out. You've got a few options here: the "butterfly"; the "waiter's friend"; the Screwpull; the "butler's friend"; the Lever Pull and more—rather a choice, as you can see.

Finding Faults in Wine

"Yuck, this smells like an old cellar. I won't order that again." That would be a real shame, as the wine is clearly badly corked. If you'd tried a second bottle of the same wine then it probably would have been fine (unless it was a dodgy batch, which is highly unusual), and, whatever it was you had chosen, you wouldn't have been put off forever. There are claims that up to one in 12 bottles of wine are corked. But what does corked mean, exactly? It's certainly not referring to the small bits of cork you get floating around in your glass after a tricky extraction.

above Your nose will detect the musty aroma of corked wine before the glass even reaches your lips, so there will be no need to taste how unpleasant it is.

Every now and then a small amount of fungus escapes the sterilization process and remains in the cork. When the infected part makes contact with the contents in the bottle, the wine soaks up the smell: hence that moldy aroma. And hence the term, corked or corky. In tiny amounts, this just dulls the wine, but it does not necessarily make it undrinkable. Corkiness can happen in varying degrees.

In a restaurant you can just send back the wine and ask for another bottle. At home, you can return it to your liquor store or supermarket with a receipt, and they will replace it for you. It's particularly annoying if the wine was a gift, or something really rare, but there's nothing you can do but dump it and open another.

Corkiness is not all that can go wrong in a wine. If that bottle of Muscadet looks a little bit more yellow than it normally does, or that young red looks a bit on the brown side, then it has probably oxidized. Oxidation occurs when too much air has got in to the wine. If the bottle hasn't been very well kept, the cork may have dried out and shrunk a little. The wine will taste dull and flat and, in the worst case, it will smell of vinegar.

Then there's that nasty whiff of rotten eggs you get in wine sometimes, which is not to be confused with the whiff of burnt matches—sulfur dioxide—which usually clears up after the wine has been open for a while and exposed to the air.

Almost every winery in the world uses sulfur dioxide. It is often added to freshly picked grapes, and it is added to the wine at the bottling stage to keep the wine fresh. No, rotten eggs is a sign of something more sinister, of hydrogen sulfide. This can form during fermentation and is a sign of bad winemaking.

Wine should be bright and clear. There is a trend for unfiltered wines these days, and these can look a tad murky, but in rare cases murky means a dose of bad bacteria. But don't jettison that old bottle of Burgundy you've been saving just because it looks cloudy after you've plucked it from your cellar—it just needs to stand upright for a bit until the deposit settles, then decant it, and even strain the last bits through a piece of fine cheesecloth if there are a few mouthfuls left.

White crystals at the bottom of a glass of white wine? No worries. They are called tartrates and they are natural deposits. They don't harm you and they don't spoil the taste of the wine either.

WINE FAULTS: CAUSES AND SOLUTIONS

Fault	Cause	Solution
corkiness	fungus	return bottle
oxidation	air	dump bottle
sulfur	too much added	give it air
hydrogen sulfide	nitrogen deficiency	dump bottle
cloudiness	bacteria	dump bottle

Decanting

Decanting wine is only really necessary when there is heavy sediment at the bottom of the bottle. Heavy sediment occurs only when the wine is pretty old. The sediment —or lees—is so fine in old red Burgundy, for example, that almost half the bottle will be undrinkable if it isn't poured properly. If the wine has been laying on its side (as it should have been, if properly cellared) then you need to stand it up for a day or two before drinking it to let it settle.

After uncorking, pour the wine in a slow, steady stream into the decanter. Stop when you see the sediment begin to work its way into the neck of the bottle (you might need a torch or a candle to light your way here). Usually there's not much wastage, but if there's more than half a glass, strain the remainder through a piece of fine cheesecloth.

So old wines aside, why do people decant relatively young wine? Decanting can make a chewy, tannic, young wine taste a bit suppler. How so? It's a matter of oxygen. Pouring the wine from the bottle into a decanter or jug exposes it more to the air. The wine can breathe again—the flavor and aromas can show off, especially for a more mature wine.

However, decanting doesn't really make a difference to cheap wine. The same reasons apply for letting undecanted wine breathe. But don't leave old wine exposed to the air for too long, as it might end up losing all its flavor.

left Decanting is essential only for old wines with heavy sediment.

What about the temperature?

A decanted or undecanted red wine left by the fire or radiator to warm up a bit is of no use at all. It'll just taste jammy and muddy. Conversely, an over-chilled white is another mistake—you just end up losing its aromas and flavors completely. If this happens, cup the bowl of the glass with your hands for a minute or two.

So what is the perfect serving temperature? For crisp, dry whites, sparkling wines, very sweet wines, and rosés—no higher than 45°F/8°C. But for bigger Chardonnays, aromatic Alsace wines, and blousy Viogniers, a touch warmer (up to 50°F/10°C) wouldn't hurt. It also depends on the weather. Generally, white wines drunk in winter are better slightly warmer than the super-cool white wine drunk in the heat of the summer.

Reds, on the other hand, should be a lot cooler than your centrally heated home —about 63°F/17°C—so ignore that serve at room temperature suggestion you see on back labels. Some lighter, fruitier reds —Dolcetto, Beaujolais—are best served slightly chilled.

You're in a hurry? For whites, those gel-packed jackets that live in the freezer are the most effective way of chilling a bottle of white quickly. Failing that, use an ice bucket filled with ice cubes, water and a sprinkle of salt (to help the ice melt more quickly). You can do the reverse for a cold bottle of red plucked from the cellar: fill an ice bucket with warm water (70°F/21°C) and submerge the bottle for eight minutes.

below An ice bucket—with a little salt added to an ice and water mixture—is a speedy way of chilling a bottle of white wine.

Eating Out

Everyone has got a nasty tale to tell about ordering wine in a restaurant: the sniffy wine waiter who rubbished your suggestion that the wine was corked; the sniffy wine waiter who suggested a bottle twice the price of your original suggestion; the sniffy wine waiter who, well, just sniffed at you when you stumbled over the pronunciation of a wine. Sniffy wine waiters have got a lot to answer for—or rather had a lot to answer for. Thankfully, those days have almost gone. There's a younger, more eager crowd out there who are only too pleased to show off their wine list.

Wine has never been so popular. This is reflected in restaurants' wine lists up and down the country: by the range that is offered and the wines that are available by the glass. There are even wine flights available: a line-up of little tasting measures of a particular variety or region that introduces you to unfamiliar wines.

Though we've still got a long way to go. The mean 6 oz Paris goblet, with its thick, unsightly rim, is still around. As is the no-info wine list—you know the one: no vintage or producer specified, littered with spelling mistakes, badly dog-eared and nothing available by the glass.

But let's concentrate on the positive. It's your wife/husband/sister/father's birthday and you've picked a restaurant that looks decent enough. First, look at those glasses. They've got long, slender stems, generous bowls and no lip—good sign. Here comes the menu and the wine list. If you've gone really classy and there is a wine waiter on hand—use him—let him know the kind of wines that you like and what you want to spend. If he is good, he will do the rest.

The six of you have chosen your food. You pick up the wine list—it has fifty wines, a good number. Just about right, in fact, unless you particularly enjoy a (long) read, flicking through page after page of region after region.

The vintage, producer, grape variety and region are all there, so is a good selection by the glass. Another Brownie point. There's a bit of blurb about each wine—though not too much—just what the wine tastes like. Great, this will help you match up the wine with the food you have chosen. You decide on an Australian Sémillon for your appetizers, and a glass of New Zealand Pinot Noir for the game terrine that your sister/brother/ mother is having.

The house red—a Chilean Merlot— looks like it will tackle all the main course dishes. You are shown both bottles. You check the vintage and the producer. You're offered a taste. A good sniff first (you'll be able to tell if the wine is corked; if it is, the waiter will replace it (graciously), then a quick slurp. The Sémillon is a little too warm. The waiter brings an ice bucket, filled with a mixture of water and ice cubes. After a few minutes, the wine is ready to drink (don't leave it in the ice, it will get too cold). The red is tasting good, too, with lots of bright, upfront, black cherry and blackcurrant fruit—an easy, textbook New World Merlot. This is how it should be.

This is how it shouldn't be: no information about the wine on the list or from the staff; you are challenged if you complain about the wine; when you ask about alternatives to your favorite style of wine, you are offered something much more expensive; you are palmed off with a different, more inferior vintage than the one specified on the list; even though you ordered the wine, it is not presented to you; there are only two bottles under $20.

CHOOSING WINE IN A RESTAURANT

1 Think about your food first, then choose your wine.

2 Use your wine waiter, tell him or her what kind of wine you like and how much you want to spend.

3 You could try the house wine first—if it's good, the rest of the list should be good.

4 If your choice of food varies, don't worry about finding a wine to match, there are plenty of good all-rounders from the New World and Alsace whites go with most things.

5 If the list isn't up to much, stick with wines from California, Australia, or Chile, they are probably the most reliable and the best value.

6 If there is a good selection by the glass—use it. Try experimenting with a bit of food and wine matching, and go for things you don't already know.

7 Check the temperature of the bottle; if it's too warm, ask for an ice bucket.

on the case

Armed with a few nuggets of wine knowledge, you can start to

cruise the shelves at your local wine store with confidence—just

don't go and spoil it by not being able to decipher a wine label.

New World wines are relatively easy, once you've mastered the

different grapes; it's the Old World you've got to watch. Sinking

your dough into an expensive bottle of Bordeaux that is far from

ready to drink with dinner is not only a huge disappointment but a

waste of dough. And while you're at it, you might as well find out

which wines age best. You've exhausted the choice in your local

store? Well, there are numerous other outlets to buy wine—from

surfing the net to buying direct. Now you've got the wines that you

want, where do you store them? Keep turning those pages.

How to Read a Label

The label tells you a great deal about the wine. It should feature the year, the region, the wine's classification, the producer's name and address and the alcohol level.

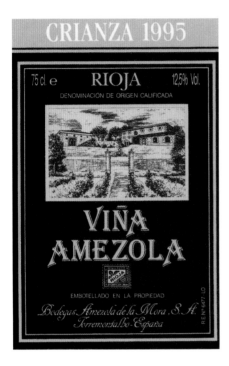

Viña Amezola, Rioja, Spain

The largest lettering on this label is the brand name of the wine, Viña Amezola. The producer's name is at the bottom, Bodegas Amezola de la Mora.

Directly above the pretty picture is the appellation, Rioja, with the words, Denominación de Origen Calificada underneath—or DOCa. It's a new, top level category, adding a fourth tier to the Spanish wine classification system, and equates with Italy's DOCG. Embotellado en la propiedad means "bottled on the estate." In the case of Rioja, the word *crianza* denotes a wine that may not be sold until its third year, and must have spent at least 12 months in oak.

Domaine Rollin, Corton Charlemagne, Burgundy, France

Burgundy labeling is a minefield for the uninitiated. The producer's name (Domaine Rollin Père & Fils) is at the bottom of the label. Corton Charlemagne is one of the grand cru vineyards of the Côte de Beaune. This label tells you this is a grand cru wine, but doesn't have to state which village it belongs to (Ladoix-Serrigny). Note that *mis en bouteille* is not followed by *au domaine*, because it has not been bottled on an individual estate, but by a négociant (merchant) based elsewhere.

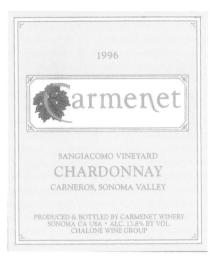

Carmenet Chardonnay, Sonoma, California

Actually Carmenet is a Médocain synonym for Cabernet Franc, but don't let that confuse you; it's also been adopted as the name of this Californian winery. In the United States, a wine labeled with one variety like this has to have a minimum of 75% of that grape, so there may be other grapes in it, but 95% of all the grapes used have to be sourced from the vineyard stated on the label (Sangiacomo Vineyard).

Bouchard Finlayson, Missionvale Chardonnay, Walker Bay, SA

Once you get out of Europe, wine labels start getting a lot easier. This South African wine simply tells us the name of the estate (Bouchard Finlayson), the vintage year (1998), the grape variety (Chardonnay) and the region of the country in which it was grown and produced (Walker Bay). "Wine of Origin" is the rough equivalent of the French *appellation contrôlée*.

Bindella, Borgo Scopeto, Chianti Classico Riserva, Tuscany, Italy

Reading down from the top we have the name of the vineyard (Tenuta Borgo Scopeto), then the *appellation* or *denominazione* (Chianti Classico, the heartland of Chianti). Then the quality level, in this case it's Italy's highest: *Denominazione di Origine Controllata e Garantita* (DOCG). *Riserva* denotes a wine that has been aged longer before being released. Then we have the producer's name (Bindella), followed by the information that the producer has bottled the wine at the estate.

Alois Lageder, Pinot Bianco, Alto Adige, Italy

Just to confuse you, here's a wine from Italy that says Südtirol (South Tyrol) on the label. Yes, the Tyrol is in Austria, not Italy. But this part of the country, the Trentino-Alto Adige, in the north, was ceded to Italy only after the First World War and most of its inhabitants—who still speak German and enjoy some autonomy—call it Südtirol. At the top in the largest letters is the producer (Alois Lageder). The grape variety is Pinot Blanc (Pinot Bianco in Italian, or Weissburgunder in German).

Domaine des Marroniers, Chablis, Burgundy, France

Chablis is one of the most famous whites, but it comes from a tiny area. Thought you'd seen a lot of it about? The name has been much abused over the years, taken without permission by producers from the United States to Argentina and used on wines that have no resemblance to the real thing. This one is the real thing; while not necessarily the best (it is *appellation Chablis contrôlée*, not a *Premier Cru* or *Grand Cru*, the next two rungs up on the quality ladder), it's usually minerally and refreshing.

Champagne Bruno Paillard, Reims, France

Champagne labels are easy. The house name dominates (Bruno Paillard), since it is a kind of brand. Reims is where Bruno Paillard is based. To the left is the style, brut, virtually the driest. To the right is the vintage. Vintage wines are "declared" in Champagne when a house feels the quality of its wine merits it, though everybody will declare in perfect years. Champagne is the

only AC wine that doesn't have to have the words *appellation contrôlée* on the label. The reference numbers to the right denote that this house is an NM (*négociant-manipulant*), ie the wine was made on site.

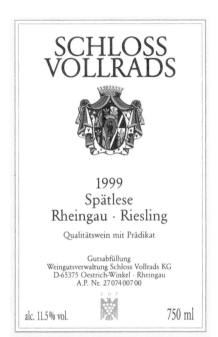

Schloss Vollrads, Rheingau Riesling, Germany

Deciphering Germany's wine labels can be tricky. But this one is a model of clarity. The producer's name looms largest (Schloss Vollrads). After the vintage, you've got the QmP category, in this case *Spätlese*, a late-picked wine, usually dry to medium. The Rheingau is one of one of the world's greatest white wine regions. *Gutsabfüllung* means "estate bottled." At the bottom is the rest of the legally required blurb: the address where it was bottled; the black eagle logo of the VDP (*Verband Deutscher Prädikats und Qualitätsweinguter*), an association of top estates and a sign of a good producer.

Château Grivière, Cru Bourgeois, Bordeaux, France

The brand name is Château Grivière, and the first line tells us that it was bottled on site. The producer is C.G.R, in Blaignan. We've also got the AC—Médoc. But then what's this—*cru bourgeois*? It's a Médoc thing. A category of red wine properties —or *crus*—designated *bourgeois* (middle class), a social tier below the supposedly aristocratic *crus classés*. They vary from simple smallholdings to fine châteaus, and there are some 300 of them.

There's even a pecking order of *cru bourgeois*, starting with the best quality, *crus bourgeois exceptionnels*, then *crus grands bourgeois* and finally *cru bourgeois*.

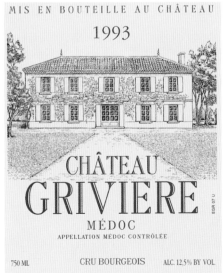

Vintage

Vintage refers to two things: the physical process of grape picking and winemaking; and the year that produced a particular wine. In the northern hemisphere, the vintage also refers to the growing cycle of the vine. In the southern hemisphere, when the grapes are picked at the beginning of the year, it refers to the year in which the grapes were picked. Simple.

When wine buffs talk about "a good vintage" it means everything conspired (climate, winemaking, vineyard management) to make high quality wine.

When wine doesn't have a vintage indicated on the bottle, it's more often than

above Season of mists and mellow fruitfulness in a Piedmont vineyard.

not inferior to one with a vintage—many table wines from the EU and jug wines in the United States are not vintage dated. The exception to the rule is Champagne, where nonvintage can still be top quality.

Why no vintage? Well, winemakers are playing it safe by mixing in some of the previous year's wine with the current year's wine to achieve a consistent—if sometimes dull— house style. By law, a vintage-marked bottle of wine must have 75 percent (or 85 percent in some countries and regions) of that particular year's harvest,

above Protecting ripening grapes against the weather, especially in Europe, is essential.

Where to go for information

Wine magazines publish their own vintage charts. But beware, some are too broad in their overview of the dozens of micro-climates—with their own particular variations —that exist within regions. One of the best is Robert Parker's very detailed *The Wine Advocate Vintage Guide*, broken down by country, region and grape variety, (www.wine-advocate.com).

giving the winemaker at least a certain degree of flexibility when the going gets tough.

Vintage is all-important—or it was, up until a few years ago. Winemaking techniques have advanced so much that even in a bad year, it's possible to make a decent wine. That said, in Europe, at least, things get very tricky when the elements play up.

A tricky growing season directly affects the wine's structure and its aging potential. A dry hot summer, for example, could cause alcohol levels to soar, while a soggy harvest can result in thin wines. Combine all this with its appellation—or terroir (see page 173)—and the wine's fate is determined.

New World countries have it easy, mostly. There's not much vintage variation in, say, Chile or Australia. Not like Europe. If you're in a restaurant with a questionable wine list, opt for a wine from either of these New World countries, you won't go too far wrong. But go for an unfamiliar name in Burgundy from the 1994 vintage, for example, and you might come unstuck.

If you are rather partial to Burgundy —or Bordeaux or Piedmont—it's worth familiarizing yourself with the vintages. It could save you a lot of disappointment.

Even in a particular year and region, the quality and character of wine can vary hugely between producers and properties. This is where the professionals come in: evaluating wine at its difficult, infancy stage, predicting, as best they can, its likely characteristics and ageing potential—a vital service when buying *en primeur*.

And remember, if it was a textbook year for an early-ripening grape, such as Merlot, it may not have been quite the same story for a late-ripening grape such as Cabernet Sauvignon, when rain fell in the latter end of a particular harvest.

In short, there are many variables. But, hey, this is what makes wine so much fun.

right Inspecting late-ripening Nebbiolo grapes, destined to become bottles of Barolo.

Buying wine

above Knowledgeable staff in a well-stocked wine store can make choosing new wines a little less daunting.

How you buy your wine is a matter of personal preference; each method has its own advantages and disadvantages in terms of convenience and choice so it is worth considering all the options.

The supermarket

When you're faced with a whole shelf of unfamiliar names, buying wine can feel a bit like a lottery. This is especially so in a supermarket, where staff do not specialize in wine and so are not able to help in the selection. If you want this kind of advice, it is best to seek out an independent store that specializes in wine—a search on the net may locate one near you. Go armed with a list of questions.

That said, the supermarket is a source of incredible value for money where wine is concerned (producers tremble at the sight of supermarket buyers, knowing that they demand the lowest possible prices), and if you do your research, there are many bargains to be had. Even if you don't, it is very rare these days to land a totally dud bottle. Winemaking and vineyard practices have advanced so much that it's quite difficult to make a really bad bottle of wine.

You can make life easy and just go with the point-of-sale promotions that highlight a particular wine or flag up the latest medal or magazine tasting score that a wine has notched up: at least you know that, at worst, the wine will be a pretty decent glug.

Study the back labels—these get better and better, and will give you an indication of the style of the wine if you are not familiar with the grape varieties and what food they should be drunk with. Most supermarkets indicate levels of sweetness, or style, so it's pretty hard to make a big mistake.

If you want to splash out on something special, it is probably better to save your money for the specialist merchants who offer mail order—most have good websites. The rather warm, bright, supermarket shelf is not the best storage condition for a fine wine, and the vintages on offer will invariably be too young and far from ready to drink.

You can keep an eye on the specialist food and wine magazine recommendations —let the objective professionals taste for you. But be quick if there's a real song and dance, because the wine will disappear off the shelves quickly.

Or you can do your own research (as you are doing right now)—read wine books, wine magazines, newspaper articles on wine, and browse the Internet to gen up on the subject. Armed with even a little knowledge, a trip to your local store or supermarket will be loads more fun. Some of the better main drag wine stores will hold regular in-store tastings. These are a great way of finding the wines you like, so use them. Staff will probably have attended at least one wine course, and should be well-versed in less mainstream wines, which is, after all, the edge that the chain wine store has over the supermarket.

Look for familiar names and grape varieties, but be open-minded about trying unfamiliar and unusual wines. You can give yourself a price limit to focus your choice —but don't be afraid to blow it every now and again—think how much you sometimes spend on single items of food.

Buy by the dozen—it's cheaper—but try the wine first and check that you are not being fobbed off with a not-so-good vintage, or that it has been stored badly (indicated by, for example, weeping corks). The same goes for "bin-ends" sales—but if there's a bargain in there, buy big.

If the wine is faulty, don't drink half of it before deciding whether it really is corked, or oxidized; take it back as full as possible.

The specialists

So we're getting a bit choosy now, are we? The main street has lost its appeal? Want something a bit more special? And you want some service, please. The independent wine store is what you want. If you're lucky enough to live near a good one, then you'll know what I'm talking about: it has row upon well-kept row of well-sourced wine from good vintages; it has seductive lighting and well-designed display areas; a special room for the rare stuff, with the rest of the wines—not on sexy display—lying down in temperature- and humidity-controlled storage facilities out the back. The staff are full of suggestions for the Thai-French fusion dinner party you are about to throw; they open a bottle of something for you to taste, before they let you buy a mixed case; they usually deliver free and lend you glasses—you're in wine store heaven.

There are plenty dotted about the country and more are opening as interest and demand grows, just have a look on the internet, you'll get a surprise. Depending which state you live in some will deliver nationally (if you order one case or more), others will deliver in the immediate area (though that could mean up to a 50-mile radius) and many offer mail order.

below Specialist merchants and independent wine stores will usually deliver wine by the case—and it's more economical, too.

Wine clubs

You haven't got time to browse, and you would rather do it from the comfort of your own home? Then join a wine club. Members order wine by mail from helpful catalogs and receive information about each wine and its producer in a regular newsletter, plus they get invited to the occasional dinner or tasting. You sometimes get the chance to buy *en primeur* (see overleaf) and you are encouraged to buy mixed cases. The downside is that many wine clubs' wines are pretty mainstream (because they are the easiest to sell), and you can't taste before you buy, which means, of course, that you miss out on the whole touchy-feely thing: checking over the wine to make sure that it is not past its prime. You can find details about wine clubs on the net in national and local newspapers, in wine magazines and through wine stores.

The Internet

Wine on the web is big—and it'll get bigger. There were a few hiccups in the early stages and some wine sites have already bitten the dust—but it's here to stay. There are many sites on alcoholic drinks, but there are, literally, thousands of wine sites.

The web has inspired everyone from the wine buff and his amateur "hobby" site to the fusty old wine merchant. The most successful companies will be those that manage to combine the traditional elements of wine retailing with all that the net has to offer. Some will be new names, others will be newly web-savvy trusted merchants.

Who's looking? It appeals to many, from the casual drinker, looking for the best bargain on the supermarket shelf, to the serious collector in search of something rare.

Net benefits

When would we use it? What's wrong with nipping down to the supermarket or your local wine store? Or mail order, come to that? Here are some of the main advantages: you don't have to move from your desk—just tap in a region that takes your fancy, or set a price limit, or pick a style (or specify all three) and you should be presented with a range of wines that meet your criteria (if you're lucky there will be tasting notes too). This should be followed by swift delivery, at your convenience within your state's liquor laws. Prices are sometimes lower; choice is sometimes greater; the potential for customer feedback is huge; and your supermarket's shortcomings (shelves of wine with unfamiliar names, no information from the staff) will be—or are already—superseded by its dynamic online search facilities, bags of information, and home delivery.

And what about hassle-free auction bidding for the budding collectors among you? There are many on-line wine auctions— even traditionalists such as Sotheby's (www.sothebys.com) are doing it.

Expert information

But can you ask a computer questions like, what can I serve with pumpkin pie? Yes, you can. The better wine sites offer a question-and-answer service via email, with access to the kind of experts you wouldn't find in your local wine store or supermarket.

The web is a great source of information for all. It's an unbeatable educational tool to improve wine knowledge, with direct communication between producer and customer (winemakers can now receive direct feedback about their wines). As

well as order wine, you can visit virtual wine regions, such as South Africa's www.wine.co.za or www.winepros.com.au for Australian wines, and check out the latest on vineyard fire or frost damage; you can study the experts' tasting notes on the current vintages; read the latest US and UK wine magazines; you can even learn how to make the stuff—and all in one sitting.

Many sites, such as www.wineaccess.com, offer forums for their users. These offer surfers the facility to post and reply to messages. While the advice offered by others might not always be from experts, useful information can still be gleaned and it also makes visiting sites a more interactive and enjoyable experience.

above Not only can you find out lots of information about wine from the web, you can also buy wine at on-line auctions.

One of the great advantages of the net is its search engine feature. Anyone searching for fine and rare wines—say, a bottle of vintage port from your father's birth year for his 60th birthday—can now trawl the brokers and merchants. If you know the wine, but you don't know who sells it, no worries, there are sites such as www.winesearcher.com that detail hundreds of merchants worldwide. Same story if you've enjoyed a wine in a restaurant and want to find out where to get it. Don't know which site to go to? Check out the information in www.bestwinesites.com

left Buying wine still in the cask and a year before bottling is risky, but can be rewarding in more ways than the purely financial.

When to buy

Only in the best vintages, and only for the best wines; anything else is a rich man's folly. Keep an eye on those vintage reports.

What to buy

I would advise, mainly, red Bordeaux classed growths and good *crus bourgeois* (see page 70); classed growth Sauternes; Northern Rhône reds and whites; red and white Burgundy from top producers; vintage ports; top estates in Napa, California; and a selection of very big names in Italy.

En primeur

Buying wine before it's even bottled may seem like a risky thing to do, but it's common practice with wines from Bordeaux and, increasingly, with a handful of other wine regions. The wine trade term for this wine sold as futures is *en primeur*.

By buying the wine early, you not only secure sought-after wines, you also pay less —or that's the theory. It has its advantages when supply exceeds demand, as it did, rather dramatically, in the Champagne-swilling 1980s. On the negative side, when the economy takes a dive, wine prices may level off, or even fall. Currency exchange rates can change. Or worse, the middleman (between you and the producer) may go under, leaving you with a barrel of nothing.

There's also the question of taste: trusting your investment to a third party's tasting assessment of a single cask sample, slurped six months after harvest and a year before bottling, is risky.

How it works

Cask samples are traditionally shown in the spring following vintage. Sales are negotiated through brokers and buyers. You cough up as soon as the price is fixed but only get the wine two years later, having paid the duty and all the shipping costs, of course. A producer usually only releases a small part of its total production *en primeur*, depending on his cash flow and the hunger of the market. And it's the producer who sets the price.

How prices are decided

It depends on the vintage. If it's a good one —a great one—the wines will sell far better than wines from a difficult vintage. Then there's the whole hierarchy thing: the pecking order of the numerous crus also affects the price. When a producer steps out of line and gets greedy (charges too much) and then the wine doesn't measure up two years later, his or her reputation suffers.

How it began

This way of buying wine has been happening for a while in the wine trade, but only taken up by consumers recently. The *en primeur* system was established between château owners and buyers (the *négociants*) to help cash flow (château owners must sit on their wine in barrels for two years before bottling, tying up a lot of their cash).

Direct and at auction

You could get close up and personal with producers and get to know—if you really want to—every stage of your wine's growing history if you choose to buy direct.

But you can't just roll up to any old château with your car trunk open wide—especially if you are in Bordeaux. Most top-classified growths in Bordeaux can't be sold directly to the public anyway—the wines go through a négociant. The rest is by appointment only. It's the same story in Burgundy, though things are changing slowly. But outside these regions, you will find a more open-door policy.

Outside Europe, it's a completely different story. In Australia, for example, most wineries have a tasting area open to the public most days of the week. You can taste before you buy, and you can often get wines that aren't available elsewhere.

If you want to make this a regular occurrence, not just a vacation thing, it starts to get tricky. It really only pays if you're going to regularly drink—or sell—large amounts (you may have a little café or restaurant, say, and you want to source a house wine yourself). You may save 10–15 percent, but on the minus side, there's a mountain of paperwork (customs forms, shipping cost calculations), heavy import duties and taxes, the risk of theft, damage and faulty wines (with no after-sales service), and other such headaches like some US state liquor laws, where it is illegal for consumers to buy wine direct from outside the state. Most small wineries aren't equipped to handle small international orders. If you really want to keep buying your proud discovery, approach a wine merchant with whom you do lots of business and get them to order it (but you'll still have to pay near-retail prices).

At auction

Wine auctions are places where you should definitely not get carried away. Before you know it, you've paid double the retail price for a first growth Bordeaux (see page 96). But don't worry—if you're the excitable type, you can mail, fax, or even email your bid.

If you do your homework, buying wine through auction can make sound economic sense. Everyday wine is not seen here, but it is also not just rare bottles from sought-after vintages either: it's possible to find current or recently released wines in an auction catalog for less than at your local wine merchant. Try to stick to a price, and remember to check out in advance the on-top costs like sales tax and so on.

How do you know the wine will be in good condition? Because the auctioneers are usually wine experts and will have checked the wine's provenance thoroughly: how long the wine has been held and where it was originally bought. The same rules apply if you decide to sell wine through an auction (you must check the legality of this in your state): an auctioneer will reject it if it hasn't been stored (in a temperature- and humidity-controlled cellar) correctly.

The Price of Wine

What makes one bottle of wine cost $50 and another $10? How can one bottle of wine reach $36,000 at auction (as it did at Sotheby's New York on 19 November 1999, for a single bottle of 1811 Château Lafite)? The price of wine is dependent upon many factors: the cachet of the region/producer/vintage (the level of greed too, or the excessive hiking of prices in the belief that it automatically buys respect and prestige); the price of the grapes and the labor costs; the heavy repayments on that new computer-controlled fermenter—or new winery, come to that; the pricing policy of the producer and/or merchant; the cost of transport, bottling, labeling, marketing—not to mention any duties and taxes.

So, do wine prices reflect quality? Well, the answer has to be no, not necessarily. All manner of factors can affect the price of wine: some countries' production costs are much lower than others (South America particularly so); currency fluctuation (which is not always passed on to the consumer); and political events (the fall of communism in Eastern Europe left a wine mountain in countries such as Bulgaria and Hungary), to name three.

Take the grapes themselves, too. Prices are normally fixed annually to take into account supply and demand, as well as vintage characteristics. Grapes are normally bought and sold according to variety and sugar content—remember that most of the

world's wine grapes are not estate grown, but vinified independently of the grower.

In most regions there is a representative body, which oversees grape prices, although in the US individual growers can negotiate with individual wineries. Sugar content is the most common measure of quality—for example, the best grapes grown in cool climates are those with higher must weights, an important measure of grape ripeness (warm to hot climates, though, have no problem getting their sugar levels up, so other factors will then come in to play).

The more go-getting wineries reward growers for producing good quality fruit. Some wineries will vinify these grapes separately, commanding higher prices for the wines made from the best batch of grapes from a particular vineyard.

And talking of vineyards, the price paid for the land itself is yet another cost factor.

The region—or even the vineyard—has a major effect on the quality of wine, and as a general rule the higher the quality of the wine, the higher the price of the land. The cost per hectare varies hugely around the vinous globe: for a good site, already planted, in the Napa Valley in California, you're looking at upward of $225,000 per hectare (1ha=2.47 acres); suitable vineyard land on Australia's famous terra rossa soil in Coonawarra is over $55,000 per hectare.

Even Argentina is no longer a cheap option—land prices in Tupungato, a hot new cool climate area in the Mendoza region, has seen prices leap (and rising still) from $500 per hectare to $5,000 in under five years as foreign investors fight over prime land.

below The quality of wines sold at auction is virtually guaranteed, but the price will depend on a complex mix of factors.

Storing and Organizing Wine

Picture the scene: you've just tasted a wine in a restaurant on vacation. You liked it very much, so you buy a couple of bottles from the supermarket/airport/wine store to take home and save for a special occasion.

A few months—or more—later, you pull the cork and pour out a glass for your friends, the story of when you first tasted the wine still fresh in your mind. Ugh! It smells and tastes like vinegar—and all because you stored the wine incorrectly. What a waste. If you had followed a few simple rules, you could have avoided that disappointment.

below The kitchen, with its constant changes in temperature and humidity, as well as the chances of direct sunlight, is definitely not the place to store wine.

When to keep wine

These days, most wine is made to drink young. Why? Because over 90 percent of all wine is drunk within forty-eight hours of being bought. Not many people keep wine any more. But with interest in wine snowballing the way it is, it won't be long before every one of you is digging out a cellar in your back yard.

Winemaking techniques have changed. The main aim now is for maximum fruit and minimum tannin, so there's no need to wait five years or more for the wine to be ready to drink. Indeed, the longer you leave most wine these days, the worse it gets: all that fresh, zingy fruit just dies away if left in the bottle for too long. Only the top ten percent of all reds and about five percent of

all whites improve after five years, and only a tiny one percent has the ability to go the full decade or more.

So how do you know what wines should be kept and what should be drunk?

The back label on a bottle is pretty good at giving advice on when to drink the wine. But what about more expensive wines? Your local wine store or supermarket invariably doesn't go in for cellaring, but did you realize that this means the most expensive wine on these shelves will probably give you the least pleasure that evening? They need time and are far too tannic with little fruit just yet.

Generally, the rule is, the more expensive a bottle, the more it will repay in terms of aging: after five years, or more, the balance of fruit flavors and bottle-aged characters in the wine will taste far more delicious. Though having said that, a few of you might prefer the tannic, bold, primary fruit of a young Cabernet. Ultimately, it comes down to personal choice.

Where to keep wine

Fact: how you store wine will affect how the wine ages. If the temperature is constantly changing and the wine is exposed to light, it will age the wine prematurely. If wine is exposed to extremely cold temperatures for several months, the wine won't develop properly. Extreme heat, too, causes untold damage (for example, pallets of wine left on baking tarmac en route from winery to merchant) for the bottles can "weep" (wine seeps out through the cork), forever damaged.

A bit fickle, isn't it? Well, yes. Wine is a living, breathing thing and how you treat it affects its taste. We're not talking about

A QUICK GUIDE TO STORING WINE

WHITES TO KEEP FIVE YEARS OR MORE

Sémillon
Riesling
Chenin Blanc from the Loire
 (late harvest versions of the latter
 will age even longer)
Botrytized sweet wines
Grand cru white Burgundy

WHITES TO DRINK IMMEDIATELY

Most inexpensive varietals
Most vins de pays
Rosés
Asti and Moscato Spumante
Anything that says "table wine"
Anything in jugs, boxes, or cans
Manzanilla and fino sherry
Albariño
Pinot Grigio
Many Italian whites
Portugal's Vinho Verde

REDS TO KEEP FIVE YEARS OR MORE

Shiraz
Nebbiolo
Many Portuguese reds
 – especially those from the Douro
Madiran
Médoc
Graves
Cabernet Sauvignon
 – especially Californian
Hermitage
Supertuscans
Brunello di Montalcino
Barolo
Barbaresco
Amarone
Ribera del Duero
Vintage port

REDS TO DRINK IMMEDIATELY

Anything that says "table wine"
 or vins de pays
Anything in jugs, boxes, or cans
Nouveau wines
German reds
Alsace reds
Loire reds
Dolcetto
Lambrusco
Many Eastern European reds
Ruby port

above Standing bottles upright in your cellar must be avoided at all costs, and humidity and temperature need to be carefully controlled.

wine kept for drinking the following day or week (though an afternoon left in a hot, sweaty car doesn't do it any good), but about wine that you want to hang on to for a bit. This could be for a few weeks or a few years.

How, exactly, it develops in the bottle is still a bit of a mystery, but research has shown that temperatures below 41°F/5°C and higher than 68°F/20°C are a threat to its development. So it follows, then, that if you store wine at a higher temperature it will mature more quickly. That's not to say you should stick a tannic wine that you are itching to drink somewhere warm to "help" its evolution. Nor should you leave those bottles on top of the refrigerator—as many

mistakenly do—where there are frequent blasts of hot air and a constant vibration (or even worse, by the stove). Cooler temperatures, a bit of quiet, and somewhere dark is what wine really wants.

How cool? Below normal room temperature. The ideal temperature for wine is between 50 and 59°F/10 and 15°C. If you are lucky enough to have a cellar, then of course there will be some seasonal variation, but this won't affect the wine so much as a daily swing in temperature. The wines will continually expand and contract in their bottles and the corks will suffer, eventually leaking and leaving a thick, syrupy goo around the edge.

If you have invested in one of those temperature-controlled cabinets in which to store your wine, then you'll have no worries on that score. But if it's a cellar or a space under the stairs, then it pays to invest in

a thermometer. Locate any hot or cold spots and insulate accordingly.

Humidity is another important factor in a wine's evolution. Not for the wine so much as for the cork. That's why you lay bottles on their sides: the cork might shrink —dehydrate—if there's not enough humidity. The wine's contact with the cork helps prevent dehydration too. If you decide to take things really seriously, the ideal humidity level in a cellar should be about 75 percent. Too much humidity and the labels fall off and your racks will rust. If it's a bit too fuggy down there, locate the damp spot and seal with resin or cement flooring with a polyurethane seal against moisture —or cover the floor with a layer of dry sand. Not humid enough? Then buy a humidifier, or improvise with a bowl of wet sand.

Why does wine need darkness? All light harms wine—sunlight especially. It dries

above Store bottles on their sides to keep the wine in contact with the cork and so help prevent it from drying out and shrinking.

out the cork, fades the labels and ages the wine too rapidly. Remember this the next time you have the urge to pluck a fine wine off that brightly lit store shelf.

Storage possibilities

Not many of us are lucky enough to have a cellar. Modern homes don't make it easy to keep wine because central heating or, worse, a baking (or freezing) attic plays havoc with wine kept for more than a couple of weeks. So what is the best thing to do?

In a small apartment or house you can adapt almost any unused corner—a cupboard, an old closet, under the stairs—to wine storage. Just make sure it's dark, cool, humid and far from any vibrations (such as refrigerators, generators, heaters and the like). Lay the wine on its side to keep the corks damp and swollen, which preserves the airtight seal.

No available space? Then buy a wine storage cabinet from a specialist manufacturers. The cabinets are about the size of a refrigerator, but are 39°F/4°C warmer, and they can store up to 250 bottles. Some models allow you to store wines at several temperatures—the coolest on the bottom for long term and a serving temperature on top for everyday use. Alternatively, beg a friend to let you use a corner of his or her cellar (think of "caging" the wines with a lock and key, just in case they are tempted to help you drink it!)

You want to store more than 250 wines (but still have no cellar space)? Okay, then rent space with the professionals, either with the merchant you bought the wines from or with one of the specialists in wine warehousing. You'll be charged a storage fee, depending on how much wine you have (and what your relationship is like with your merchant), and you must get insurance. Make sure your wine is stored separately from the merchant's own stock and that it is clearly identified. Obviously, you will only be able to dip into your hoard when the shop or wine warehouse is open, so it makes sense to lay down wines that are far from ready to drink, and keep a stock of the wines that are ready to drink on hand at home.

You could also turn a small spare room into a walk-in cellar (very swanky)—insulation made from polystyrene panels will maintain cellar temperature. Or you could buy a very big temperature-controlled wine cabinet (a tad expensive).

You've got a yard? Dig a hole and drop in a ready-made "spiral" cellar. The Spiral Cellar was invented in 1978 by Georges Harnois. It's made of precast concrete and comes with steps and bottle racks and it is not as costly as you would think. Underneath the garage is a good place, or outside shed.

What about the garage as a place to store wine? Fine, if you just make sure it is well insulated from temperature change and odors. Finally, definitely do not use the outside shed.

Organizing your bottles

This section is for those of you who have decided to take things a little more seriously on the cellar front. Here are a few tips on organizing your cellar—whether you have decided to go for 200 or 2,000 bottles. You have endless options, even organizing wines by their style: meaty reds; light reds; sparkling wines; aromatic whites; crisp dry whites, and so on, so that when you have decided what you are going to cook, the right style of wine is easy picking. Alternatively, you could organize your wine according to region.

Whichever way you go for, remember to place wines that need a bit of aging on the bottom, or in that awkward-to-get-at-space, and those wines that are ready to drink in the most accessible place.

If you have enough wines that need serious aging, then consider storing them in their own space altogether. You can even squirt the label with fragrance-free hairspray to seal against the damp.

The most popular and inexpensive way to store bottles is in wooden racks connected by galvanized metal strips in

a modular system, although you could opt for wood or terracotta. Old-fashioned cellars have "bins"—large shelves on which you pile the wine as many as ten bottles deep. People used to buy their wine in barrels and it was all the same, so this was a convenient way to keep the bottles. Of course, we don't buy this much wine today. Most of us buy a case at most, more often just a single bottle of a particular wine.

Keeping the books

What is the point in cellaring wine if you can't find it? Get a cellar book going. It should lead you straight to the bottle you are looking for and remind you what grape varieties are in it, what you ate with it, when you last tasted it and what you thought of it. You could get really thorough and include yields and vinification details. Your cellar book can also tell you where you bought it and why, how much it cost and what the critics said about it and when they —or you—considered it ready for drinking.

And remember that the size of the bottle can also determine the time it takes to mature: if you've bought/been given a

above Wines in your cellar can be organized by region, or even by style and it is a good idea to place those ready for drinking in the most accessible place.

magnum (1.5 liters) or another big bottle —known collectively in the trade as large formats—then you need to know that the wine evolves more slowly in these than in a regular 75 cl bottle—or more quickly in a half bottle (37.5 cl).

Wine also ages better in magnums, though we don't really know why that is. Some say it's the greater contact with the air (because of the bigger volume), which slows down the maturation process. Giant Champagne bottles, on the other hand, are more about marketing than better evolution (anything above a magnum tends to be filled with wine made in smaller bottles). And talking of size—the biggest bottle is a Nebuchadnezzar, a 20-bottle capacity monster found in Champagne and Burgundy.

And, just to confuse things, a double magnum is known as a *jéroboam* in Champagne, but a *jéroboam* in Bordeaux is known as a *rehoboam* (the next size up) in Champagne.

the
wine
world

Wine reflects the place it is grown, so join a whistle-stop tour of the wine world, kicking off in the United Kingdom. The UK is not a major player, but it's trying hard—and the bubbly isn't bad. Then, it's off to France, on through Spain, Italy, Portugal, Germany, Austria, a quick trip through Eastern Europe, the Middle East and on to South Africa and Australia, before we have a fling with New Zealand and a foray into Central and South America. Then we head to the United States and Canada, finishing up with a round-up of other countries. Some countries on our journey include a regional spotlight that uses the icons below to show the kinds of wines the selected regions are famous for.

Red   White   Rosé   Sparkling Sweet   Fortified

England and Wales

Don't laugh, but England can make decent wine. In fact, England can make fantastic wine. Sparkling wine, anyway. If you've never tried it, now's the time. England has naturally well-drained chalk soils, and a climate that provides high acidity.

Red wine? That's another story. There are increasing quantities of cool climate-loving Pinot Noir for England's sparkling production, and decent still wines made from the grape are now beginning to emerge. But give it time for more experience to be gained, and you may be looking at some classy wines.

Winemaking isn't new to England. By the eleventh century there were at least 38 vineyards, some as far north as Yorkshire. Worcestershire, too, was renowned for its wine—imagine, Cuvée Malvern.

The Romans probably introduced vines to England. They certainly made wine out of the grapes, judging by the pottery drinking cups unearthed in settlements. Vines flourished in England until the climate started to change.

By the fourteenth century, summers were wet and cloudy. Then Henry II acquired Gascony with his marriage to Eleanor of Aquitaine—and the Brits never looked back. Until 50 years ago, that is.

England's first commercial vineyard was established in Hambledon, Hampshire, in

right There are no officially demarcated wine regions in Britain, but vineyards, indicated here by dots, are to be found in only England and Wales.

above Harvesting Pinot Noir grapes on the rolling North Downs at Dorking, Surrey.

The grapes

The most planted grape varieties are Müller-Thurgau, Reichensteiner and Seyval Blanc, but they are gradually being replaced by Chardonnay, Pinot Blanc, Bacchus, and Dornfelder (coming into its own). A handful of varieties make up the rest from Schönburger to Pinot Noir. Red grapes tend to struggle to ripen because of insufficient sunlight, and growers have to rely on viticulture techniques, such as plastic tunnels.

The regions

There are no officially demarcated wine regions in Britain, but grapes are grown in England and Wales only—as far north as Durham and as far south as Cornwall. Although there are vineyards in all but six English counties, most tend to congregate in the southern counties of England and Wales. Site selection and canopy management (see page 153) are the keys to winemaking in England and Wales. The main moan is not enough sun and too much rain, so anything that can be done to adjust these rather important weaknesses is done.

The quality

Official classification of English and Welsh wines was introduced in 1992 with the Quality Wine Scheme. Wines that gain this status can use the words "English Vineyards Quality Wine psr" (or Welsh Vineyards Quality Wine psr) (psr means produced in a specific region) on the label. Under European law hybrid varieties (eg, Seyval Blanc) are not permitted to gain quality wine status, so in 1997 the Regional Wine Scheme was introduced; those wines that make the grade can carry "English Counties Regional Wine" on the label.

the 1950s, and the rest followed. There are now 872 hectares of vineyard, and about 114 producers, with an industry that is becoming increasingly more professional in both its methods and attitudes—and consequently becoming attractive to tourists on the vineyard trail.

An increasing number of English and Welsh wineries have opened up a restaurant or café on site, in addition to the winery shop, plus vineyard tours and a valuable (and sometimes hands-on) insight into wine production.

Although it has done little until now to encourage twentieth-century English viticulture, the British government has even contributed its first subsidy—tiny though this subsidy may be.

There is a typical flavor in English whites—elderflower, apple, and gooseberry, with a twist of grapefruit on the finish. Some wines are made "off dry," although drier styles are on the increase. There's a bit of oak-aging too, though this is generally less successful, as it overwhelms the delicate fruit. Winemaking methods here are much the same as they are in any other country in northern Europe.

France

France has been knocked off its perch. For many years, centuries even, the big names in the classic regions in France had no competition; until the rest of the wine-drinking world discovered that there is life beyond Bordeaux and Burgundy. New World wine producers are stealing a march on their mentors, with easy-drinking, reliable wines. The French, after a spot of navel-gazing, are finally responding. They've cleaned up their cellars, installed stainless steel tanks and now use the latest gizmos. Result? A vast improvement in French wine across all levels.

The grapes

There are many grape varieties used in France and they differ from region to region. Here are some of them.

Most red Bordeaux is made from a blend of three to five red grapes: Cabernet Sauvignon; Cabernet Franc; Merlot; Petit Verdot, and Malbec. Whites include Sauvignon Blanc and Sémillon. In Burgundy, Pinot Noir, and Gamay rule, while Chardonnay reigns supreme over the whites. All Champagne is made from just three grapes: Chardonnay, Pinot Noir, and Pinot Meunier. There are 13 grape varieties grown in the Rhône, including Syrah, Grenache, Mourvèdre, and Viognier. A mixture of French and German varieties are used in Alsace, among them Gewurztraminer, Riesling, and Pinot Gris. The Loire uses some grapes from Bordeaux, and some from Burgundy, including Sauvignon Blanc and Cabernet Franc.

The regions

1. Bordeaux
2. Burgundy
3. Champagne
4. Alsace
5. The Loire Valley
6. The Rhône Valley
7. Jura and Savoie
8. Southwest France
9. Languedoc-Roussillon
10. Provence

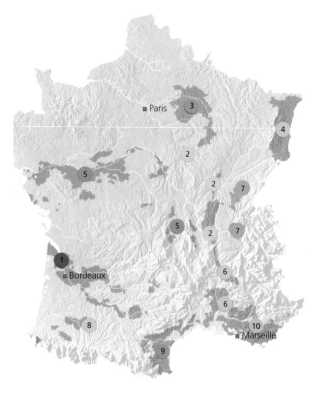

There are many grapes used in Southern France—key reds include Cabernet Sauvignon, Merlot, and Mourvèdre; key whites include Sauvignon Blanc, Petit and Gros Manseng.

The regions

France has virtually every grape-growing condition you could ask for, from the cool, chalky-soiled north to the sunny, thyme-scented south.

Champagne

Let's start in the north, in the Champagne region. It's funny to think that without the bubbles, Champagne would be undrinkable. Its northern latitude means the grapes, even when fully ripe, still have high levels of acidity. But combine the still wine with yeast and a tiny amount of sugar and you've got something with finesse and balance. Made in the hills around the towns of Reims and Epernay, the Champagne region

above The vineyards of Provence are carved out of limestone and cleared pine forests. The region produces some classy wines as well as Côtes de Provence for glugging.

is divided into four main areas: Montagne de Reims; Côte des Blancs, Vallée de la Marne, and the Aube. Champagne is almost always a blend of grapes from these areas. The sparkle, according to the history books, was a mistake initially. In the 1660s, a Benedictine monk called Dom Pérignon couldn't control the wine's fermentation because of the unpredictable weather and he kept getting a persistent sparkle. Much to his horror, Paris society loved it.

The mainstay of any Champagne house is its nonvintage. The object is to keep a uniform style, which is achieved through blending several vintages. Vintage Champagne is "declared" in the very best years. *Deluxe cuvées* use the best wines for blending, and come in fancy bottles with fancy price tags.

left The neat, hillside vineyards
and fairytale buildings of Alsace
are reminiscent of a German landscape.

Alsace

Drive on farther east, and you hit Alsace.
It looks nothing like Champagne, with its
densely wooded hills and Hansel and Gretel
villages. More German, in fact – and you'd
be right to make the connection because it
was part of Germany for a time, finally
returned to France after the Second World
War. The wines reflect its mixed history
and are made from largely German grape
varieties. But they're different from German
wine: higher in alcohol and drier. At their
best they have a distinct flavor of the *terroir*
(see page 173), and the soils in Alsace are
incredibly varied. The best are classified as
grand cru. *Vendange tardive* are the delicious
late-harvest wines, while *Sélection de Grains
Nobles* are the best sweet wines, but rare and
expensive. Alsace can make good bubbly
too, called Crémant d'Alsace.

The Loire

Heading south from Paris, you hit Tours
and the Loire—with the longest river in
France, and the grandest châteaus. The
Loire wine region divides roughly into four
areas: Muscadet at the river's mouth; Anjou;
Touraine; and the Upper Loire, each with

their own distinctive style. Muscadet is
neutral and low in alcohol, perfect with the
local oysters. Best to go for are bottles with
Muscadet de Sèvre-et-Maine on the label,
and always look for the words *sur lie*; they
mean that the wine has been kept on its
lees, which gives it more depth. Forget
Anjou Rosé, go instead for Anjou-Villages
and Anjou-Blanc. The best reds in Anjou,
though, are those from Saumur-
Champigny. In Touraine, go for reds from
Bourgueil and Chinon, or for sweet wine
choose Vouvray made from Chenin Blanc.
The Upper Loire is the home of the
famously pungent wines from Sancerre,
and Pouilly-Fumé, while Menetou-Salon
and Reuilly are similar, but lighter.

Burgundy

Burgundy has the most complicated of all
the classification systems and it would take
a lifetime to understand the nuances of
its terroir. Put simply, there are general
appellations (see page 172), such as
Bourgogne Rouge, and regional
appellations, such as Chablis. Village wines
come next, naming the best villages, such
as Meursault. Next up is *premier cru*, the
second-best vineyard within each village—
the village comes first on the label—like
Meursault-Charmes. Finally, *grands crus*, the
top wines in Burgundy, from the top vineyards—they even dispense with the village
name on the label. Because the vineyards
are in the hands of numerous smallholders,
the négociants used to rule the roost here,
but now the best wines come from growers
who bottle the wine themselves.

The uniqueness of Burgundy is the complexity of its geology, with startling differences between wines grown in close proximity. Red Burgundy varies from light, perfumed redcurrant fruit (from villages like Santenay) to full, sturdy, blackberry fruit (Gevrey-Chambertin). The best white Burgundy achieves great structure, from the rich lushness of Meursault to flinty Puligny- and Chassagne-Montrachet.

The Burgundy region starts in the far north with steely Chablis. The Côte d'Or is the central part of the region, running south from Dijon to Santenay. This is where the greatest red and white Burgundy is made—in and around modest villages and small towns, such as Beaune. South of the Côte d'Or is the Côte Chalonnaise and the Mâconnais, producing soft, easy-going fruit. Beyond here is Beaujolais, where the best wines (the *crus*) achieve depth and substance—and nothing like the nouveau wines you might already be familiar with.

Before we leave central France, it's worth pointing out the Jura and Savoie wine regions near the Alps to the east. Jura's whites, in particular, have a distinctive nutty tang, while Savoie has an interesting variety, called Altesse.

Northern Rhône

On to the Rhône. The river boasts vineyards on its banks for almost its entire length—from its source in the Swiss Alps to its mouth near Marseilles. The variety of wines, predictably, is staggering. In wine terms, the valley is split into the northern and southern Rhône. The vineyards in the

right Saumur is the main wine town on the Loire and home of several major wine companies.

north are positioned on steep, granite terraces and they make some of the river valley's best wines: Côte-Rotie, with its fragrant Syrah, is now as expensive as top Bordeaux and Burgundy. You can choose between the individual styles of Côte Blonde and Côte Brune. A little farther on are the two small white ACs (see page 97) of Condrieu and Château-Grillet. Both grow the cult Viognier grape, with its luscious apricot fruit. Next up is St-Joseph, which makes slightly lighter, softer red than Côte-Rotie.

Hermitage and Crozes-Hermitage follow. The former makes one of the world's greatest red wines—Syrahs that need a decade or more to open up fully. The dark, rich wines of Cornas are mini-Hermitages. St-Péray finishes the northern Rhône with, oddly, a talent for sparkling white.

Southern Rhône

The landscape changes dramatically in the southern Rhône. Flat plains fan out as far as the eye can see. The wines are different too. Fruit—a whole basketful of different

varieties—ripens easily in the baking summer sun. Most southern Rhône wines come under the Côtes du Rhône appellation. They can be red, white, or rosé. Next step up in quality is Côtes du Rhône-Villages, from 16 different villages. The most prestigious appellation in the south is Châteauneuf-du-Pape, making raspberry-packed reds, and a handful of peachy whites. Gigondas also makes good reds and rosés, with Vacqueyras close behind, while Lirac and Tavel are famous for their rosés. If it's an apple-scented sparkler you want, then you could try Clairette de Die, made in the isolated Drôme Valley.

above Grenache Noir, the most widespread grapes of the region, flourish in the inhospitable sun-baked stony soil of the southern Rhône.

Bordeaux

Bordeaux is the biggest producer of fine wines in France. The reds are the most famous (with the British especially) and the best are used as a benchmark the world over. But the region is suffering. Negative press (from mostly UK critics) about the region's soaring prices at the top level and about the quality dive at the lower end of the market (not to mention increasing competition from the New World) has led to falling sales. Things are finally changing. The Conseil Interprofessional du Vin de Bordeaux (CIVB), the regulatory organization responsible for the wines of Bordeaux, announced that they are shaping up.

The Gironde river flows through the heart of the region. Just a quick look at the names of châteaus—Smith-Haut-Lafitte, Lynch-Bages, Palmer—gives you some idea about the history of the place, about the English, Scots, and Irish families who set up trading companies here, then started to grow vines. Bordeaux even belonged to the British at one stage—for 300 years from

1152, when Henry II married Eleanor of Aquitaine. It was after the Dutch drained the marshes that became the vineyards of the Médoc in the seventeenth century that things really began to take off. That was when the grand châteaus were built.

The wines vary hugely. One hectare of vineyard can differ wildly from its neighbor, because of choice of vine variety, difference in climate and soil, and, of course, the personality of the château owner. Bordeaux Rouge and Bordeaux Blanc are the basic appellations, with Bordeaux Supérieur subject to slightly more rigorous regulations. Then there are large areas—like the Médoc, the Graves and Pessac-Léognan, St-Émilion—each with its own AC, and smaller ones too, like Pomerol.

Bordeaux also has numerous classifications. In 1855, the leading châteaus of the Médoc were classified into five levels by Bordeaux' wine brokers—fifth growths through to the top level first growths in ascending order or quality—plus a Graves property, Haut Brion. Below this is Crus Bourgeois (see page 70).

Provence

There's much more to Provence than the cheery rosé that you may well have quaffed on holidays in the region. In fact, things have been improving here pretty quickly. There are now some ambitious producers, turning out classy wines. You just have to look at what's happening in Bandol. Some of the best wines in the region come from this tiny appellation. It makes dense, truffley (if expensive) reds and characterful rosé. Côteaux Varois is also turning out some decent wines, as are the Provence appellations of Cassis, Bellet, Palette, Côteaux d'Aix-en-Provence, and Les Baux-de-Provence. Most wine from Provence, though, is labeled Côtes de Provence, but you have to look hard for the good stuff. While we're down here, it's worth giving Corsica a mention. The craggy, mountainous island has improved its winemaking, recently, with good stuff from appellations such as Patrimonio and Ajaccio.

Languedoc-Roussillon

It may be best known for producing gallons of cheap wine, but Languedoc-Roussillon has been producing some rather fascinating wines of late. The region stretches from Montpellier to beyond Perpignon, and covers the Aude, Gard, Hérault, and Pyrénées-Orientales *départements*. Great wines are starting to emerge, some made from traditional grapes such as Syrah, others from Cabernet Sauvignon or Chardonnay, using the *Vin de Pays* regulations to get around the restrictive AC rules.

right Hérault in the Languedoc has more vineyards than any other *département* in France.

Other Southwest regions

The reds and whites of Bergerac and Buzet are made from the same grapes used in Bordeaux, and compare in quality, but are cheaper in price. If you like tannins, choose Cahors, though they are more approachable than they were in the past. Gaillac comes in all colors, but the whites are the best known. Madiran makes interesting reds from Tannat, while Jurançon makes fascinating whites, from dry through to sweet.

Quality

There are four main French wine classifications. The largest and supposedly the best is *Appellation d'Origine Contrôlée* (AOC or AC). It means the wine comes from where the label says it does, and is made from the approved grapes. Next is *Vin Délimité de Qualité Supérieure* (VDQS), with similar restrictions but for regions not classified as AC. Then comes *Vin de Pays*, or country wine, which states on the label where it's from and sometimes the grapes from which it is made, used by enterprising winemakers in the south to avoid the constraints of AC rules. Finally, *Vin de Table*, table wine, can be made from just about anything, from anywhere, without indication of vintage.

BANDOL

The jewel in Provence's crown, the tiny appellation of Bandol makes the region's best reds, and some of the best rosés. The wines are dominated by the Mourvèdre grape, which inexplicably shines here (it's a workhorse grape at best elsewhere), with flavors of truffle and mushrooms underlying the dense black fruit. The appellation is named after the port from which they were once shipped all over the world. The vineyards are on south-facing terraces, protected from the cold north winds. Other grapes are grown here, namely Grenache and Cinsaut, used for the herby rosés. Whites are made here too, but the reds are where it's at.

Mourvèdre vines flourish on the terraces of Château la Rouvière.

PESSAC-LÉOGNAN

This is the best bit of the Graves, the large Bordeaux appellation that lies south of the city, with its trademark gravelly soils. The Pessac-Léognan appellation is relatively new, created in 1987. The name comes from the two most important communes and includes all of the properties named in the 1959 Classification of the Graves. The wines are distinctive. Reds are mainly Cabernet Sauvignon, with some Merlot and Cabernet Franc thrown in. Tasting notes range from smoky bacon to warm bricks. The whites made from Sauvignon Blanc and Sémillon grapes, grown on the sandier parts of the vineyard, are powerful and can go a decade or longer.

The red wines of the region are mainly Cabernet Sauvignon.

CHÂTEAUNEUF-DU-PAPE

Châteauneuf-du-Pape produces the best wines in the southern Rhône. When it's good, it's really good, with dusty, soft raspberry fruit. The wine takes its name—it means Pope's new castle—from the relocation of the papal court to Avignon in the fourteenth century. A papal vineyard soon followed. Thirteen grape varieties are allowed to be grown here, though Grenache is the top dog. It dominates plantings on the poor soils and produces wines that combine concentration with the usual sweet fruit of Grenache. There is a white version, using Grenache Blanc and other grapes, but it's relatively rare and can lack acidity and fruit.

The papal château may be in ruins, but the papal vineyards continue to flourish in the rocky ground.

TOURAINE

They call Touraine the garden of France and it is the Loire's most important region, centered around the town of Tours. Touraine is famed for its reds, from the individual appellations of Bourgueil, Chinon, and St-Nicolas-de-Bourgueil, and for its still and sparkling dry to sweet whites from Vouvray and Montlouis. The climate varies considerably, with eastern vineyards distinctly continental, while western vineyards are tempered by the Atlantic. There's an equally large line-up of grapes. Generally speaking, Sauvignon Blanc and Gamay are grown in the east—the Loire's most famous Sauvignons are those from Sancerre and Pouilly-Fumé.

Freshness is the keyword for Touraine whites.

MADIRAN

Madiran is one of the most dynamic regions in France: it has turned its chunky tannic reds, into spicy, exciting wines. The traditional red grape here is Tannat, making up most of the blend. Winemakers have been working on ways of softening the chewy grape—including micro-oxygenation (a technique to control aeration of the wines in tank)—to produce wines packed with fruit that are ready to drink, but with aging potential. The whites are hot, too. They're called Pacherenc du Vic-Bilh, the Gascon name for the tangy blended local varieties, among them Courbu and Petit Manseng. The deep yellow wine can be either dry or sweet, depending on the vintage.

The wines of Madiran have been revolutionized in the last 20 years.

BEAUJOLAIS

Forget Nouveau. Instead, why not go for a Beaujolais-Villages, or even better, a cru Beaujolais? Gamay is the real star in this Burgundy appellation. It thrives in the granite hills above Lyons, with very bright, easy, drink-me fruit. At its best—a *cru*—it makes richly flavored wines, which can even improve with age (though steady—only a couple of years). There are ten crus Beaujolais: Brouilly; Côte de Brouilly; Regnié; Morgon; Chiroubles; Fleurie; Moulin-à-Vent; Chénas; Juliénas, and St-Amour. There are differences between them, but they're all made with the Gamay grape.

The church watches over the Gamay vineyards in Chiroubles, one of the top ten Beaujolais villages.

Spain

Spanish wine is not that easy to get to grips with. It's the third largest producer of wine in the world and stands alongside France and Italy in terms of complexity. But do we think of Spanish wine in that light? Do we, heck. We think we know the soft, vanilla-laden reds of Rioja—one in five bottles of Spanish wines drunk in the UK alone is labelled Rioja—and we're renewing our love affair with sherry. We've probably cracked open a bottle of two of Catalonian Cava, too. But we're only just beginning to discover the rest.

Things have changed a lot in Spain over the last ten years. The country has been pouring money into new technology and new vineyards, and has made vast improvements in winemaking. The cheap stuff has improved enormously and this is down to plenty of attractive, youthful fruit.

It always used to be wood that was admired in Spain, but it has plunged head long into modern winemaking with its abundance of shiny stainless steel. Cold fermentation and early bottling is the thing now; while long oak aging is on the way out—except for the top traditional wines. And there has been a surge in seriously fine wine coming out of Spain, wines that are making waves internationally.

The regions

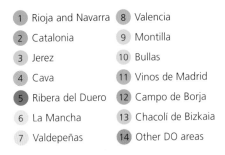

1. Rioja and Navarra
2. Catalonia
3. Jerez
4. Cava
5. Ribera del Duero
6. La Mancha
7. Valdepeñas
8. Valencia
9. Montilla
10. Bullas
11. Vinos de Madrid
12. Campo de Borja
13. Chacolí de Bizkaia
14. Other DO areas

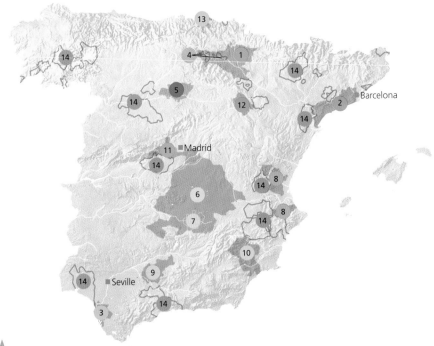

Spain's a land of extremes—from the lush greenery of the north coast to the baked white land in the south—which is reflected in her wines. They range from light, dry whites in the cool Atlantic region of Galicia to heavy, alcoholic reds in the Levante and the Mediterranean south. Then there's Andalucia, in the southwest, most famous for its sherry.

Spain may be the third largest producer of wine, but it has more land under vine than any other country in the world. It's just that the yields are so low—thanks to the arid climate.

The grapes

The country has some 600 grape varieties, but 80 percent of the country's vineyards are planted with just over 20 of them. Garnacha is Spain's most widely planted grape in the quality wine stakes. Tempranillo is the second most planted variety, with Cariñena and Macabeo close behind. Gaining ground is Albariño in

right Ribero del Duero has now become known for some of Spain's best wines.

above The 11th-century, Catalonian Castillo de Milmando presides over Chardonnay vineyards as far as the eye can see.

Galicia and Verdejo in Rueda. International varieties are also making significant inroads in some parts of Spain, notably Cabernet Sauvignon, Merlot, and Chardonnay.

The regions

There are many. Starting from the top left-hand corner, in green Galicia, the main players export-wise are Rías Baixas and Ribeiro. In north-central Spain, Rioja leads the way. Ribera del Duero now makes some of the best wines in Spain, with Cigales, Toro, and Rueda all sharpening up their act.

above International varieties such as Sauvignon Blanc have found success in Catalonia.

Top far right is up-and-coming Somontano and solid Penedès. Priorat is exciting palates with its rich reds, while farther south, in the middle of Spain's vast plains is La Mancha, with its soft, easy reds, and Valdepeñas. Topping off the hit list is Jerez, in the far southwest, with its famous sherry.

The quality

Spanish oak-aged reds are usually denoted by the words *crianza, reserva,* or *gran reserva.* The structure of Spanish classification law is more or less the same as any other EU country. Vino de Mesa is ordinary table wine; Vino Comarcal is a category of regional wines that applies to certain good-quality wines that don't happen to fall under a particular DO; *vino de la tierra* are country wines—like French *vin de pays*; Denominación de Origen (DO) is the equivalent of French Appellation Contrôlée. There are 56 of them at present, but new areas come on line every year; Denominación de Origen Calificada (DOC) is like Italy's DOCG and applies to top DOs with a history of quality. There's only one so far—Rioja.

below The combined influence on the climate of mountain and ocean plays a central role in growth and ripening in the Rioja vineyards.

RIBERA DEL DUERO

Spain's most expensive wine comes from Ribera del Duero—Vega Sicilia. Another cult Spanish wine, Pesquera, is also made here. This is red wine country—rich red wine country—using mostly Tempranillo (known here as Tinto Fino or Tinto del Pais), grown on a barren plateau between Valladolid and Aranda, near the banks of the Duero river—(the Douro, in Portugal). But whereas port has been famous for over three centuries, the success of Ribera del Duero's wines is a relatively recent phenomenon.

● Madrid

In Ribera del Duero, Tempranillo grapes are known as Tinto del País ("local red").

PENEDÉS

Barcelona ●
Ebro

Catalonia's top region, Penedés, is famous throughout the world for Cava, which can be excellent, although its blend of Parellada, Macabeo and Xarel-lo is not to everybody's taste. In addition Penedés is famous for its international style reds and whites. Producer Miguel Torres is the main man in this area, making wines from richly oaked reds to lean, lemony whites. He imported French varieties and techniques in the 1970s and the region hasn't looked back since.

Sparkling Cava is a made by the Champagne method.

RÍAS BAIXAS

Albariño is the name of the game in this region and its results are wowing visitors to wine bars from San Francisco to London. Wonderful with food and on their own, the creamy, peach, and apricot white wines are the best in Galicia, if not the whole of Spain. This is the little-known Spain of clouds and rain. You will find lush greenery everywhere you look along the many-fingered estuaries called rías. The grapes are grown on granite soils on a specially adapted vine-training system, which keeps the grapes well off the soggy soils.

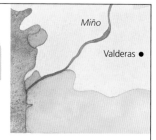

Miño
Valderas ●

Vines are supported on low pergolas in the hot warm climate of the northwest.

Portugal

For many, port is the first thing that springs to mind when you think about Portugal: that sticky, sweet drink so loved by Aunt Mabel, with a dash of bitter lemon; or the crusty colonel, in his winged leather armchair, puffing on his cigar. Or maybe you're remembering that bottle of Mateus Rosé you turned into a lamp-stand in the 1970s? Think again. Not only is port a seriously good drink to be enjoyed by all (and at all times), but Portugal also makes fabulous table wine.

True, much of the wine made in Portugal is drunk by the natives—the country has a huge per capita consumption. And most Portuguese wine is made from numerous peculiar-sounding native grape varieties. But guess what? They taste great and range from the meaty reds of the Douro to the light, spritzy whites of Vinho Verde. There has been some movement toward planting international grape varieties, such as Cabernet Sauvignon and Chardonnay, but the country's winemakers have pretty much stuck to their guns and stayed with their own grapes— concentrating instead on getting their gear up to date in the winery and improving things in the vineyards.

And finally, a word on port. Have you ever tried a ten-year-old tawny straight from the refrigerator as an aperitif? Or white port with a splash of tonic, a handful of ice and a sprig of borage on a hot, summer's day? There's much more to port than Aunt Mabel's favorite ruby.

In short, Portugal is a small country with a big future in wine, and it deserves a place in your cellar or on your table.

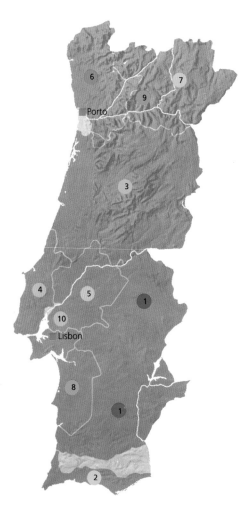

The regions

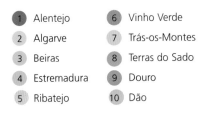

1	Alentejo	6	Vinho Verde
2	Algarve	7	Trás-os-Montes
3	Beiras	8	Terras do Sado
4	Estremadura	9	Douro
5	Ribatejo	10	Dão

The grapes

The best-known red grapes are Touriga Nacional and Tinta Roriz—famous because of their roles in port making. Others include Baga and Periquita, or the distinctive white wines made from the spicy Fernão Pires or the scented Roupeiro. The best-known white grape is Alvarinho, which makes Vinho Verde.

above The picturesque, heavy, traditional baskets for carrying freshly picked grapes down steep hillsides are no mere tourist attraction, but continue to serve a practical purpose in the Douro vineyards.

above The Douro valley produces some very exciting red table wines, but it is best known as the homeland of port.

below Port has lost its old-fashioned, dull image and is enjoying a renewed appreciation.

The regions

Starting at the top of the country, there's Vinho Verde (*verde* means green—but read youthful). The Douro is next. Below that is rather old-fashioned Dão, with Bairrada next door. Estremadura and Ribatejo follow, with lesser-known regions Portalegre, Bucelas, Carcavelos, Setúbal, Terras do Sado and Colares right behind. Finally, there is the Alentejo, and not forgetting Madeira—with its fortified wines extraordinaire.

The quality

Look out for Denominação de Origem Controlada (DOC) on the label – it signifies the highest quality level for Portuguese wines. The second tier of newer wine regions goes under the heading of Indicação de Proveniência Regulamentada (IPR). If you see the words *vinho regional*, it doesn't necessarily mean lower quality—it also means that there's a greater flexibility in grape varieties and aging allowed. The same goes for *vinho de mesa* (table wine).

DOURO

It's generally considered to be port country. The port is sweet, rich, and warm. However, several port houses now make serious table wine, which are mostly red and often command serious prices – in fact, the Douro is home to the country's most expensive red wine, Barca Velha, made by port producer Ferreira. Many of the best table wine vineyards in the Duoro valley are in the cooler west of the region or on the higher slopes, compared with the finest port vineyards, which tend to be situated in the heart of the Douro valley, on steep terraces upstream from the town of Régua.

The precipitous vineyards of the Douro are constructed on terraces.

ALENTEJO

The sparsely populated Alentejo plains cover almost a third of Portugal, stretching all the way from the coast in the east to the frontier with Spain. It now has a DOC for the better wines, plus eight subregional DOCs, including Redondo, Reguengos and Vidigueira, producing cheerful reds and whites to serious single estate wines. It also produces much of the world's cork, and cork trees dot the countryside.

Pickers carefully select ripe Trincadeira grapes on the Alentejo plains.

MADEIRA

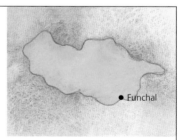

The Atlantic island of Madeira, 750 miles/1200 km southeast of Lisbon, produces some of the world's most exciting fortified wines. Grapes growing on the island's terraced volcanic slopes ripen in the humid, subtropical climate to produce a variety of styles of wine denoted by their natural sugar content. They range from Sercial grapes producing the driest wines, through to Malvasia grapes, which make the sweetest styles. The resulting raisiny fruit and naturally high acidity means Madeira keeps well in bottle.

Gentle baking in a humid climate gives Madeira its unique flavor and character.

Italy

The land of wine, that's what the Ancient Greeks used to call Italy. Nothing's changed, then. Italy still has vines everywhere, from the foothills of the Alps to the tiny Italian island of Pantelleria, off the Tunisian coast. Wine pervades every aspect of life in Italy, yet the rest of the world has only just started to take notice. Most Italians didn't really worry about the quality of their wine until recently. It wasn't until after the Second World War that Italy really started to catch up with the rest of Europe. Now Italy's top wines rival the best from

Bordeaux. It's not just the Tuscans and Piedmontese who are making the best stuff either; there are serious reds—and even whites—coming out of almost every region.

The pace of change has been—and still is—fast and furious. But not without some lawlessness. Winemakers had to break, or rather ignore, a few wine laws to get there.

The regions

1. Northwest Italy
2. Northeast Italy
3. West-Central Italy
4. East-Central Italy
5. Southern Italy and the Islands

Though that's not say there isn't still a lot of rather thin stuff around, sold under the useful names of Soave, Valpolicella and the like. The whites are generally less memorable, and there's a common thread running through most of Italy's reds—a certain bitterness —which makes drinking it solo hard going, but with certain foods they work well.

To really understand Italy's wines, it is best to think of it as a group of regions, rather than a single country.

The grapes

Italy has a profusion of grape varieties— more than any other European country. There are international varieties being used, sure, but as producers discovered French

above Chianti Classico is the heartland of the Chianti zone in the central Italian region of Tuscany.

vines and French techniques, they also discovered the benefits of their own native grape varieties.

Let's start with the grapes of the north, of the Piedmont: Nebbiolo is the star grape here, reaching its peak in Barolo and Barbaresco. Barbera and Dolcetto are popular red grapes here too, while Arneis is the region's most distinguished white grape.

Over to the east, Schiava is the main red grape of the Alto Adige, but there are a host of other interesting grapes in the northeast, including Tocai Friulano, Teroldego and

left High mountain peaks form a dramatic backdrop to the vineyards of the Alto Adige region. Once part of Austria, its wines are prized all over the world.

The quality

Italian wines are classified into four categories. The most basic is *Vino da Tavola* (VdT). Next is *Denominazione di Origine Controllata* (DOC), specifying grape varieties and viticultural and winemaking techniques. *Denominazione di Origine Controllata et Garantita* (DOCG) follows DOC, supposedly guarantees the quality and origin of the best wines. But what of those maverick producers who started to use French grape varieties and techniques? *Indicazione Geografica Tipicà* (IGT)—a new category that slips in between VdT and DOC—is a more flexible law for those who don't want the constraints of a DOC.

Corvina. Sangiovese is the big red grape in central Italy and Trebbiano is the big white. In the south, Primitivo is making waves, as is Aglianico.

The regions

Starting in the far north again, there are the Tyrolean heights of Alto Adige, with its fresh, perfumed whites. While some of the country's most exciting reds are in the Piedmont and the Veneto, in the middle of Italy, the wines swing from light, easy drinking whites such as Rome's nutty Frascati, to foamy, pungent Lambrusco. The great Tuscan reds are here too—the so-called Supertuscans—made from international varieties as well as indigenous ones, that until recently were labeled as *vino da tavola* because they flouted the wine laws. Then to the south, and regions such as Campania, which have seen significant changes of late. Here you can find big, rich, lush reds made from southern Italian variety Aglianico, the honeyed whites from local grapes Greco di Tufo and Fiano di Avellino and the nutty, buttery Marsalas of Sicily.

below The world's largest wine exporter, Italy offers a vast range of wines that are constantly being improved.

VENETO

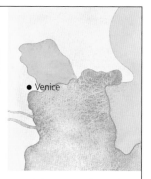

The Veneto is a huge area, stretching from the Adriatic sea inland to Lake Garda, from the peaks of the Dolomites in the north to the flat Po Valley in the south. It has been making wine for centuries and is the Italian wine industry's commercial center. Production is huge, revolving around three wines: white Soave, red Valpolicella and Bardolino. That's not to say it can't be good; there are serious wines here—labeled Classico—in all three appellations, made in the hillier bits of the region.

Soave castle overlooks the vineyards of Trebbiano and Garganega grapes that produce one of Italy's best-known white wines.

TUSCANY

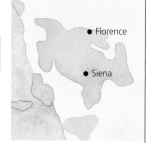

Together with its undulating hills of olives, pines, and vines, plus the odd Michelangelo, Tuscany is Italy's wine powerhouse. Its most famous white wine is Vernaccia di San Gimignano, which dates back to the thirteenth century. But reds are where it's at. Chianti is made with Sangiovese – or it always was, until winemakers started to add Cabernet, Merlot and the like. The wines were (and still are) so good that they were nicknamed "Supertuscans"—much to the annoyance of the authorities, who only let them have *Vino da Tavola* on the label.

The name Chianti, once applied to both white and red wines, is now used only for reds.

SICILY

Sicily is more dynamic than ever before, producing juicy reds and fresh whites, despite the unforgiving heat of the summer. It is also the home of smoky, sticky Marsala. Things like cool fermentation have helped, so have vineyards sited in higher altitudes, replicating the cooler conditions of the north. Sicily has many native grape varieties, and one of the best is Nero d'Avola, producing wild, herbaceous, long-lived reds. Lying just off Sicily is Pantelleria, with its appealing, honeyed, sweet passito wines made with Moscato grapes.

Once, the wines of Sicily were virtually unknown outside its own shores.

Germany

Liebfraumilch has got a lot to answer for. This bland, sweet, flowery white, that was once an easy sell in restaurants, has just about single-handedly destroyed Germany's reputation for wine. Okay, so it started out as a good idea—as an ideal beginner's wine. But most Liebfraumilch around now is nothing more than cheap sugar water. Even famous Liebfraumilch producer Blue Nun has dropped the name from its label. Thankfully, Lieb sales are dwindling, but if that's been your only introduction to date of German wine, you've been missing out.

For starters, Germany produces the finest Rieslings in the world. The country's best wines are made from this grape. They can be steely and dry, laced with apples and apricots. Or they can be richly honeyed, bursting with pineapple, peach, and mango fruits, with a satisfying twist of lime on the finish. The drier styles are fantastic food wines, coping with a line-up of different, sometimes difficult, foods. Another plus point is that these wines are relatively low in alcohol, which makes them perfect for summer drinking.

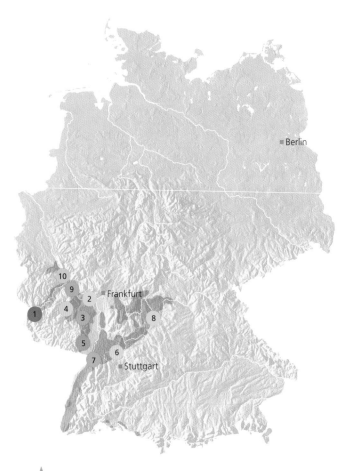

The regions

1. Mosel-Saar-Ruwer
2. Rheingau
3. Rheinhessen
4. Nahe
5. Pfalz
6. Württemberg
7. Baden
8. Franken
9. Mittelrhein
10. Ahr

above Old foundations and ancient families preserve the tradition of the characterful, fruity, perfumed wines of the Saar valley.

The grapes

Riesling reigns supreme, but Müller-Thurgau is Germany's most widely planted grape. It is high yielding and not particularly exciting, unless in the hands of an expert. Others include the more interesting Rieslaner (a crossing of Riesling and Silvaner), which makes great dessert wine in the Pfalz. Weissburgunder (aka Pinot Blanc) produces peaches and cream wines in the Pfalz and Baden. Rülander (Grauburgunder or Pinot Gris) produces spicy, dry whites and delicious dessert wines. Tricky Scheurebe, when handled with care, produces great dry wines in the Pfalz, as well as honeyed Beerenauslese. Red grapes—and gradually more are being planted here—include Spätburgunder (particularly in Baden-Württemberg) and the Beaujolais-style Dornfelder.

The regions

The Mosel-Saar-Ruwer makes fabulous Rieslings and many of the great estates are here on its steep, slatey slopes. Many of the best dry Rieslings, though, are on the sun-drenched northern slopes of the Rheingau. The Pfalz picks up the prize for the most dynamic region in Germany at present, while the Rheinhessen, on the banks of the Rhine, is the largest of the country's wine-producing regions. The Nahe is sometimes overlooked, but its wines have a pleasing mineral quality. Red wines are Baden-Württemberg's thing, while Müller-Thurgau is Franken's forte (though the best wines are made from Riesling). There are other regions, but you don't often see their wines outside Germany: among them Ahr and former East German Sachsen.

The quality

Now here comes the difficult bit: the minefield that is Germany's wine classification system. Are you ready? It's important now—get it wrong and you may find you've bought a bottle of sweet wine to go with your Friday night fish. There are six categories, and they come in order of increasing ripeness of grapes:

• *Kabinett*, made from ripe grapes and usually light in alchohol.

• *Spätlese*, made from really ripe, late-picked grapes and often a little sweet (though there are dry versions).

• *Auslese*, made from really, really ripe grapes, with a touch of noble rot and usually sweet (except in the south, where they can be fermented dry).

• *Beerenauslese* (or BA for short), made from selected, hand-picked grapes almost always affected by noble rot.

above Just under 80% of Germany's vineyards are planted with white vine varieties, with Riesling and its offspring Müller-Thurgau together snapping up nearly half of the area under vine.

• *Trockenbeerenauslese* (or TBA for short), made from individually picked grapes, affected by noble rot, and produced in tiny quantities, making some of the sweetest wine in the world (and a labor of love for the winemaker).

• *Eiswein*, is, well, ice wine—the grapes are picked frozen and pressed carefully.

But before you go, there are a couple more things to remember when reading a German wine label:

• QbA (*Qualitätswein Bestimmter Anbaugebiete*) means, literally, quality wine from designated regions, though in reality this varies from not very good to very good.

• QmP (*Qualitätswein mit Prädikat*) means, literally, quality wine with special attributes.

• *Landwein* is a table wine from 20 designated areas.

• *Deutscher Tafelwein* is the most basic table wine.

And now the Germans have introduced another classification system—Erstes Gewächs—First Growth, yes, just like in Bordeaux, and now primarily underway in the Rheingau.

left "Noble rot" weakens grape skins and concentrates the sweetness of the wine.

PFALZ

Pfalz is Germany's second largest wine region, bordered by Rheinhessen in the north and France in the south and west. The wooded hills of the Pfalz forest, which soar to 2000 ft/630 m in parts, draw many visitors. The vineyards run along a 50-mile stretch following the eastern edge of the forest, making fiery Riesling and great, zippy Scheurebe. Young guns rub shoulders with rejuvenated traditional estates. The northern part is home to many of the top names, while the south is where the new action is to be found.

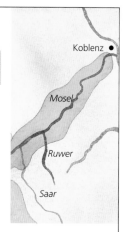

Protected by mountains and similar to Alsace, this region has a warm dry climate and benefits from a rich, fertile soil.

MOSEL-SAAR -RUWER

This is a white wine area, and the wines are lighter and crisper than many other German wines. They are generally pale and aromatic with a zippy acidity. The vineyards are situated along the Mosel river, and its offshoots, the Saar and Ruwer. Some of Germany's most famous estates are to be found here, clinging onto the steep, slaty slopes. The most significant areas to remember include Bernkastel, Piesport, Zeltingen and Erden.

Mosel-Saar-Ruwer wine is almost steely.

RHEINGAU

More of Germany's most famous winemaking estates are here, making aristocratic Rieslings. Or at least that was the story a few years back. Quality has in the meantime slipped somewhat. However, it is hoped that the introduction of Erstes Gewächs will go some way to restore reputations and to encourage others to pull their socks up. The Rheingau winemaking region stretches from east of Hochheim (this is the village that initially inspired Britain to coin the word "Hock" to describe the region's wines) to Lorch, near the Mittelrhein.

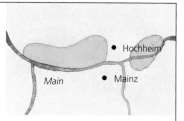

The greatest and most balanced German wines are produced in the Rheingau.

Austria

Austrians don't really make that much wine. The country produces just 0.9 percent of the world's wine. And what they do make is mostly lapped up by the domestic market. Small parcels are exported, though, and it's worth seeking them out – the top stuff especially. And prepare to be surprised; the best wines of Austria are world class.

The grapes

Forget Chardonnay, Grüner Veltliner is the white grape to watch. It is Austria's most widely grown grape and it's delicious. It comes as a zippy quaffer or a serious mouth-filler. Or how about Zweigelt? Or Blaufränkisch? Okay, so they're a bit difficult to get your tongue around, but have a go—you'll be rewarded.

The regions

1. Burgenland
2. Niederösterreich
3. Styria
4. Vienna

The regions

There are four wine zones: Lower Austria or Niederösterreich, which is the biggest and covers the north; Burgenland, in the east, bordering Hungary; Styria, a sprawling area in the south, which makes lean, acidic wines; and the suburbs of Vienna itself.

Austria is most famous for its noble sweet wines. The best come from Neusiedlersee in Burgenland. The area was part of Hungary in 1921 and the locals have a strong dialect (butt of many a Viennese joke). The lake's peculiar climate makes sure that the vineyards closest to its shores suffer the liquid-gold-giving rot. The humid mists rising off the water see to that, and in most years, producers can count on getting enough botrytis to keep the banks happy. A variety called Bouvier is the easiest grape to "rot," because it is the first to start shriveling, while the thick-skinned Traminer is the most difficult. Soils are mixed. There's loess, black soil, gravel, and sand. And

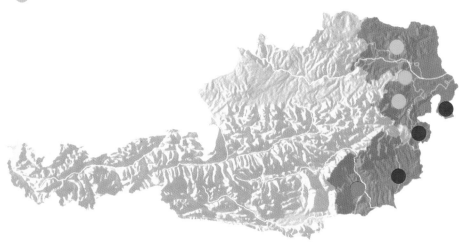

above Terraces of Riesling and Grüner Veltliner grapes flourish high above the Danube in the Wachau.

spots – the valley is 20 miles/33 km long and influenced by two major climate zones.

To the west, there's the temperate Atlantic; to the east, the warm air from the Pannonian lowlands. There are big variations between day and night-time temperatures, contributing to the exotic character of Wachau wines (90 percent of which are white). A Wachau Riesling bursts with ripe peach, apricot, and citrus fruits, with enough acidity to allow some serious bottle aging. Grüner Veltliner shines here too, and it is the most widely planted grape in the Wachau. It also does well in the clay and limestone soils of the neighboring Kamptal region.

while it's warmer here than in the rest of Austria, during the winter months the lake freezes over. On one side of the lake is the town of Rust, which has made a fortune from a particular style of (heavenly) sweet wine called Ausbruch.

The area is also becoming increasingly well known for its dry table wines. The whites are good, but the reds are the stars, made from Blaufränkisch, Zweigelt and St Laurent. The latter, in particular, has been stunning critics. St Laurent is somewhere between Pinot Noir and Syrah, with its own unique character.

Austria's best dry white wines come from the Wachau. This is Riesling and Grüner Veltliner territory. The narrow, picturesque Danube valley between Melk and Krems to the west of Vienna turns out Riesling to rival those from Mosel-Saar-Ruwer. The grapes grow on sun-kissed, vertiginous terraces of primary rock: granite, gneiss and mica schist. The drive from Durnstein to Weissenkirchen takes in some of the best

The quality

The Wachau has its own classification system: Steinfelder covers the light, fragrant whites; Federspiel is a medium Kabinett; Smaragd indicates wine from the best sites, made in the best years.

The most forward-thinking growers in the Kamptal have organized themselves along French lines: *grosse Ernte Lage* (*grand cru*); *erste Lage* (*premier cru*); and *klassifizierte Lage* (*cru classé*). Areas to look out for on labels include Heiligenstein (Holy Rock), as Riesling does well here —Grüner Veltliner even more so.

below Austria produces some world class wines, although it exports very little.

Eastern Europe

Eastern Europe has more to offer the wine lover than just cheap and cheerful wine. For example, one of the world's greatest dessert wines—Tokaji—comes from Hungary.

Hungary

Grown on the country's northeastern border in volcanic soils, Tokaji (or Tokay) is made in a completely unique way. Furmint and Hárslevelü grapes (the country has a rich stock of indigenous, unpronounceable grape varieties) are left to rot (the noble kind) in the damp, warm fall weather, then ground to paste called *aszú*. The paste is mixed with wine that has already been fermented from nonbotrytized grapes (called *szamorodni*) for further fermentation. How sweet the final wine is depends on how many *puttonyos* of *aszú* (containers of paste) are added. Three *puttonyos* make a medium-dry wine, and six a very sweet one, but all with a similar taste spectrum of apricots, marmalade, and honey. The sweetest of all, though, is Essencia, made only in exceptional years, from the juice of grapes crushed by their own weight, and used to revive the dying, so the legend goes. Hungary also makes interesting table wine out of Furmint and Hárslevelü. Both can make powerful whites, with Hárslevelü the more aromatic of the two.

Hungary's other main wine regions are the Great Plain in south central Hungary (which makes over half the country's wine),

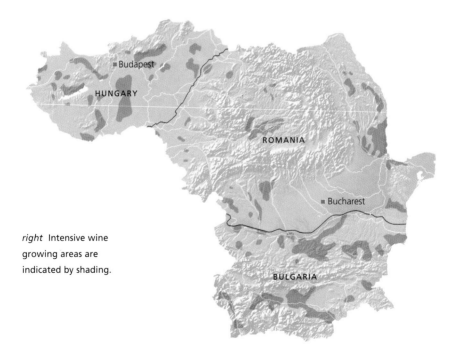

right Intensive wine growing areas are indicated by shading.

Lake Balaton, the Villány area in the south near the Croatian border, Eger and the Mátra foothills. Most of Hungary's wines are white, and are produced from more unpronounceable native grapes plus a growing line-up of international varieties, particularly Chardonnay and Sauvignon Blanc. Some new crossings, such as the Muscat-like Irsai Oliver and the spicy Cserszegi Füszeres (Gewürztraminer), are now being more widely planted for their distinctive fruit. Hungary's most characteristic red grape is Kadarka.

Soils are varied. The Great Plain is mainly sand, for example, while the area around Lake Balaton is basalt volcanic rock, with clay, sandstone, and loess. In Tokaji, the soils are volcanic with a topsoil of decayed lava.

Things have changed dramatically in Hungary over the last ten years. Up until the early 1990s, the wine industry was under state control. Then, under government

above No longer under state control, when they were immensely disappointing, the wines of Mount Lake Badacsony beside Lake Balaton are regaining their former glory.

policy, the state farms and wineries were offered up for sale, tempting foreign investors. They succumbed—to Tokaji in particular—and the massive injection of cash has resulted in a huge improvement in the country's wines.

right The vineyards of Badacsonytomaj are the homeland of many of Hungary's tongue-twisting but palate-thrilling grapes.

Bulgaria

Bulgaria has been striding ahead of Hungary. It now exports 90 percent of its wine and has recently cornered the market

above Eastern Bulgaria boasts vast vineyards growing only white grapes.

below Bulgaria has successfully rebuilt its wine industry from scratch since World War II.

in cheap, reliable supermarket quaffers. Wine is now one of Bulgaria's main hard currency-earning commodities. Its success was built in the 1980s on inexpensive varietals, especially Cabernet Sauvignon.

The country has another boast—it claims to be the birthplace of winemaking. Viniculture has been practiced in this part of the world for more than 3,000 years. It's not a big country—just 250 miles/400 km from the western border to the Black Sea and 200 miles/320 km from Romania to the north with Greece and Turkey to the south. Vines are planted all over the place, and the country's soil and climate are ideal for winemaking.

The Bulgarian wine industry, though, was in disarray not so long ago, in the early part of the 1990s after the fall of communism in 1989. Returning the land to those who could prove it was theirs was a bureaucrat's nightmare. The privatization process is still painfully slow, and the biggest threat to the

Bulgarian wine industry is the continued neglect of its vineyards.

New wine laws have divided Bulgaria into five geographical regions. These are the Danube Valley in the north, the Black Sea region in the east, the Struma Valley in the southwest and the Maritsa River and Stara Planina in the south.

Bulgaria's vineyards are dominated by international varieties, such as Cabernet Sauvignon and Merlot, plus some Pinot Noir, though if you count the wine made for the local market, there are more white grapes planted than reds. Whites, then, include Georgian grape Rkatsiteli, as well as Chardonnay and co. There is a quality scheme too, of sorts: country wines are the equivalent of French *vins de pays*; varietal wines of denominated origin are the equivalent of French VDQS, while Reserve and Special wines are superior varietal wines aged for at least two years for whites, three years for reds, and Bulgaria's best stuff. *Controliran* is Bulgaria's answer to the French *appellation contrôlée*, wines from specific varieties and vineyard sites.

Romania

Romania has the biggest potential in Eastern Europe in terms of volume. There is almost as much land under vine here as in Portugal. But it has been held back by all those years spent turning out old-fashioned wines to the former USSR. It exports only a small percentage of its production. The best regions are Dealul Mare ("big hill") in the Carpathian foothills for reds, Tirnave in the northeast, in Transylvania; Murfatlar near the Black Sea, and the oldest, and most famous wine region, Cotnari in the north, whose sweet wine was once almost as sought after as Tokaji. Romanians are particularly proud of their Cabernet Sauvignon, and they've got lots of it. But the most widely planted varieties are Feteasca Alba and Feteasca Regala, both of which produce perfumed whites of varying sweetness and quality. As a general rule, the whites are better than the reds.

below An unmistakably east European church, together with extensive vineyards, nestle in the foothills of the Carpathian Mountains in Romania.

Middle East & North Africa

As Middle Eastern and North African cooking enjoys the spotlight in restaurants and cookery books in northern Europe, it's time to look at these countries' wines, which can offer an interesting alternative to the mainstream.

Israel

The vine thrives in Israel and wine grapes grow here in five regions: Galilee in the north, including Golan Heights; Samaria; Samson; the Judean Hills, and the Negev. Most vineyards are owned either by kibbutzim or moshavim (cooperatives), with a handful of private owners. The most interesting wines currently come from Golan Heights, growing red and white grapes at high altitudes. The wine industry thrives on exporting kosher wine to Jewish communities throughout the world, as most, but not all, Israeli wines are kosher.

below Harvesting in the Bekaa Valley, home to most vineyards in the Lebanon.

The Lebanon

Think of Lebanese wine and Château Musar will immediately spring to mind. The distinctive, long aging, musky red, made from a blend of Cabernet Sauvignon, Syrah, and Cinsaut, is one of the world's most amazing wines, made by legendary winemaker Serge Hochar. The vineyards are in the Bekaa Valley, home to most other Lebanese wine producers, including Château Kefraya. They are high enough to withstand the baking Mediterranean temperatures, with mountain ranges on either side of the valley providing cool nights and rainfall. There is minimal spraying here, and most vines sprawl in bush form, though training on wires is on the increase.

Algeria

North African cooking has never been so fashionable in Europe, so it figures that the region's wines should enjoy equal attention —or at least it's worth giving it a go. Let's start with Algeria. Okay, so it's not something you see on your supermarket shelf too often (if ever), but importers are slowly making in-roads. Algeria once had as much land under vine as Germany; its wine was used as blending fodder for many French producers padding out their own bad vintages. But with the introduction of tighter controls in Europe, and an anti-alcohol Islamic government, production mostly dried up. But things have picked up again, and, with a Mediterranean climate, there are now seven designated quality wine zones, producing quaffable wines. Plantings of noble varieties are on the up, including Cabernet Sauvignon and Merlot, plus the odd bit of Chardonnay.

Tunisia

In the old days Tunisia made as much wine as Algeria, but production has now fallen away dramatically because of those pesky European wine laws. The most important wine regions are Nabeul, Cap Bon, Bizerte, Ben Arous and Zaghouan. The main grapes

above A horse-drawn plow works in Tunisian vineyards in time-honored fashion.

planted include Carignan, Grenache and Cinsaut, with a few plantings of Cabernet Sauvignon and Syrah. Most of the wines produced are full-bodied reds or light rosés. There's not much interest from foreign investors at this stage of the game.

Morocco

At least Morocco has its own appellation system, not dissimilar from the French *appellation contrôlée*. While that doesn't in itself guarantee quality, at least there are now European Union-recognized wine zones: The East (Berkane and Angad), Meknès-Fès, Gharb, Rabat, and Casablanca. Of this lot, Meknès-Fès supposedly has the best reputation for quality, with its 1,950 ft/600 m altitude.

Like Algeria and Tunisia, Morocco used to churn out the wine grapes, but with independence in 1956 came a steady decline. The state then took over the vineyards, introducing grape price fixing, regardless of quality. It has only recently loosened its grip. Private investors are now injecting some much-needed cash into its old-fashioned wineries and vineyards. Another case of "watch this space."

South Africa

The South African wine industry has got some huge changes to make—and it isn't going to happen overnight. There's still a lot of dodgy Chenin around, and Pinotage, with a few exceptions, will probably never make it big. But there's a bright light at the end of the tunnel—a new breed of South African winemaker who has familiarized himself with the rest of the vinous globe and is more open to new ideas.

The new breed isn't looking to imitate Australia or Bordeaux, as other winemakers in South Africa do. Instead, they are spending time in the vineyards of Chile and California, traveling through the Loire, Bordeaux and Burgundy, then swapping notes when they return. They are combining Old World philosophies with New World techniques to produce wines with a true South African identity.

There's a new confidence. Red grapes are being grown in traditionally white wine areas. There's also more thought going into site selection, with new areas, such as Bot River, currently being developed. There's better understanding of wood—South African Chardonnay is not the oaky monster it once was. And there's riper fruit (if higher alcohol) than ever before—with growers making sure they pick at the perfect level of sugar concentration.

The regions

1. Orange River Valley
2. Constantia
3. Olifants River
4. Durbanville
5. Swartland
6. Walker Bay
7. Paarl
8. Stellenbosch
9. Worcester
10. Robertson
11. Klein Karoo

Cape Town

While the rest of the developing wine world was working on its international varieties, South Africa was concentrating its efforts on a grape of its own invention, namely Pinotage—a cross between Pinot Noir and Cinsault, created in 1924 by a South African viticulturist.

But Pinotage has not had the best press in recent years, and only a handful of winemakers can get the best out of the grape. The obsession with it has hampered the country's efforts with other red grapes, and although there are sought-after labels now coming through, they are mere drops in the country's 70-million-case ocean.

It's not that South Africa is new to winemaking, either. It started out in 1656 using imported rootstock. But diseased vines and inferior clones have held things up somewhat, as has the obsession with Pinotage and the international boycott during apartheid. Ask anyone when the turning point came for South Africa's wine industry, and they'll reply, unanimously, "1994, Nelson Mandela."

above Paarl (meaning "pearl" in Afrikaans) provides almost perfect conditions for growing grapes.

The grapes

White wines still dominate in South Africa – though the trend is now in favor of reds. Vineyards are planted with 75 percent whites, 25 percent reds. Chenin Blanc still rules the roost, though vines are being ripped out to make way for more international varieties. Colombard is close on its heels, then comes Chardonnay, with

below South African viticulturalists are now experimenting with many grape varieties other than the ubiquitous Pinotage.

Sauvignon Blanc right behind. Riesling and Sémillon are some way behind them, with Gewürztraminer and Viognier the new kids on the block.

South Africa's reds, until recently, were dominated by Pinotage. At its best, it has rich aromas of ripe plum, with chocolate-covered cherries and cinnamon spice on the finish; at its worst, think baked nail polish. Cabernet Sauvignon now leads the way, followed by Pinotage, Cinsault, Merlot, and Shiraz, with small pockets of grapes like Pinot Noir and experimental plantings of grapes such as Nebbiolo.

The regions

Grapes are now grown in more than 50 declared "regions," "districts," and "wards." There are almost 5,000 farmers cultivating 100,000 hectares of land under vine. Production is handled mainly by 82 estates and 70 cooperatives, with new wineries going up all the time—backed by foreign investors, the odd IT billionaire, and dis-illusioned gold-mine owners from the north.

The Cape area produces most of the country's wines. The Boberg region includes the districts of Paarl and Tulbagh. The Coastal region is home to Durbanville, Stellenbosch, Constantia, and Swartland. The inland Breede River Valley region encompasses Robertson, Swellendam, Tulbagh, and Worcester. The main wine districts, though, are Paarl and Stellenbosch.

below Traditionally a region that produces white wines, Robertson is becoming increasingly known for good reds.

ROBERTSON

This is predominantly a white wine area. It's hot, dry, and fertile and makes big Chardonnays on its stony, lime-rich soils. Most vineyards edge the Breede River, which runs through the region, though many vineyards are now moving up into the cooler hills. Growers work together, swapping ideas, and regularly scoop awards for their wines. As well as Chardonnay, the area makes great Muscats and Sauvignon Blanc, and there are now an increasing number of good quality reds emerging, with Shiraz leading the way.

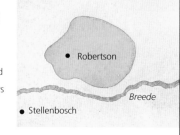

Chardonnay grapes are harvested on the Graham Beck Winery's Madeba Farm in Robertson to make big wines.

STELLENBOSCH

This is the very heartland of South Africa's wine-making industry. It boasts the greatest (and indeed still growing) concentration of wineries as well as the country's classiest wines. There are vineyards all over the region, planted from the valley floor to the rugged mountain slopes. There are about 50 different soil types, and as many microclimates. Consequently, there's not one particular style to characterize this region. Traditionally, Stellenbosch was revered for its red wines, but some stunning whites are made here too, particularly Chardonnay and Sauvignon Blanc.

Chardonnay is fast becoming as renowned as the traditional luscious reds of Stellenbosch.

CONSTANTIA

Edging Cape Town's smart, southern suburbs, Constantia can make world-class Sauvignon Blanc, which performs extremely well here, plus Chardonnay and Cabernet Sauvignon. This is where Governor Simon van der Stel established the first Cape vineyards in 1685 and set about making sweet wines. It's on the southeastern side of the Cape Peninsula, facing the Atlantic Ocean, cooled by breezes from two sides. This helps to slow down the grape-ripening process, giving wines of great concentration and finesse.

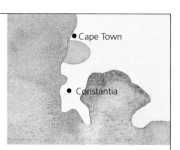

Constantia is a first division viticultural area, focused on fine wine production since the earliest days.

Australia

Who hasn't bought a bottle of Australian Chardonnay? It's everywhere—in every wine store, on every supermarket shelf, in every cellar. The Australians have done more than most to promote this grape. But lately, we've been getting a little bit bored with it. The more mainstream brands taste rather samey to our now rather grown-up palates. It seems we've moved on. The Australians' response has been to stop planting and to get regional.

Big wine companies are launching new wines that reflect the *terroir* better. These new wines are more subtle in the oak department and let the character of a particular area shine through. It's the same story for reds. The Australians recognize (along with everybody else) that red wine is what people now want, so they are turning out even more of its star grape Shiraz, as well as the equally impressive and tasty Cabernet Sauvignon.

So it's out with homogeneity and in with diversity, a diversity of styles from a diversity of regions. Alternative white varieties are also being explored—Sémillon and Verdelho, for example, which both do very well in the country. In short, Australia is not standing still—which is why it was such a success in the first place.

The regions

1 New South Wales
2 Victoria and Tasmania
3 South Australia
4 Western Australia

The grapes

If you thought Australia was all about Chardonnay and Shiraz, think again. There are about 75 grape varieties grown in Australia—divided roughly half and half between red and white.

Shiraz is the big red. Known as Syrah elsewhere, it performs brilliantly in Australia. Planted in cooler areas it's full of earthy, licorice, and leather fruit. It's less complex grown in the heat, but still offers sweet, ripe fruit.

Cabernet Sauvignon is another star red for Australia, standing alone, or blended with Shiraz, Malbec, Merlot, and Cabernet Franc. It's grown everywhere. In the cooler climates it's herbaceous and grassy, while under the hot sun, there's a mixed bag of red fruit, often smothered in chocolate. An increasing number of producers are making use of old Grenache and Mourvèdre (known as Mataro in Australia), and steady progress is being made with Pinot Noir. Sangiovese and Nebbiolo are also making more of an appearance.

Chardonnay leads the way for whites, with Sémillon (written as Semillon in Australia), Verdelho, Viognier, Sauvignon Blanc, and Riesling all on the increase. Not forgetting the Muscats, which can make heavenly dessert wines.

The regions

Climate is regarded as being more significant than soil in most regions of Australia. And boy, do the climates differ. From the wet, damp Adelaide Hills to subtropical South Burnett. Wine styles are just as varied, from the complex, multi-layered Chardonnays from the Indian Ocean-splashed Margaret River, Western Australia, to the gutsy Shiraz from the olive-tree-fringed McLaren Vale.

New South Wales

The Hunter Valley is NSW's most famous wine region. It produced the first commercial Chardonnay way back in the 1970s, though it's now Sémillon that shines, especially with a little age. Just across from Hunter is Mudgee (it means "nest in the hills" in Aboriginal), which makes great Shiraz, and good Cabernet Sauvignon.

High-altitude Orange is on everybody's lips at the moment. Other regions include Cowra, Hilltops, Riverina, and bubbly-savvy Tumbarumba.

South Australia

The bulk of South Australia is bag-in-box territory, producing more than half of the country's wines, though it also produces some topnotch stuff from prime grape-growing areas. Riesling (and Shiraz) is Clare Valley's thing.

The Adelaide Hills makes crisp Chardonnay and Sauvignons, while wines from the Barossa vary from neutral whites from the hot valley floor to fabulous old-vine Shiraz up in the hills.

above Australia has seen the future—and it is red. Cabernet Sauvignon is racked off at the Trentham Estate on the Murray River.

The Eden Valley, a cooler subregion of Barossa, competes with Clare for the best Rieslings. McClaren Vale has something for everybody, while Langhorne Creek has Jacob's Creek, the most successful of all the big name brands. Farther south is Coonawarra, home of elegant Cabernet and great Shiraz. Padthaway to the north is just as cool, and makes celebrated Chardonnays. Other areas include Limestone Coast and Eyre Peninsula.

Victoria

Once, gold brought people to Victoria. Now it's wine, from value-for-money quaffers from the Murray River, to the luscious Liqueur Muscats of Rutherglen. The latter produces a fair line-up of table wines, from beefy Shiraz to sun-kissed Semillon.

Across the center of the region are several smaller regions, including Grampians, known for its bubbly; the Pyrenees, with its gut-busting reds; the concentrated, long-lived reds of Bendigo and Heathcote; and Goulburn Valley, with its flagship Marsanne.

The other main regions are Geelong, Macedon, the Yarra Valley, and the Mornington Peninsula.

Western Australia

Some of the country's top producers are at Margaret River, Western Australia's jewel, making powerful, elegant reds from Cabernet through to Zinfandel, and voluptuous whites from Chardonnay, Sauvignon, and Sémillon.

Tasmania

The geography of cool climate Tassie swings from dense eucalyptus forest to alpine meadow. There's a distinctive style to Tasmania's wines: the fruit is far more restrained compared with the mainland. The wines are more subtle and delicate, more European. All the familiar classics are made here, from grapes grown in vineyards in the warmer, drier eastern half of the island, at low altitudes. Chardonnay and Pinot Noir reign supreme.

Queensland

The wine grapes are planted in vineyards high up in the cooler hills—in the Granite Belt, to the west of Brisbane. South Burnett is the newest, prettiest Queensland region.

The Quality

Produce of Australia is the most basic classification; South-Eastern Australia, used for mass-market blends; State of Origin with a number of zones, regions, then subregions. The top wines can be labeled outstanding or superior.

ORANGE

Up until recently, Orange was a well-kept secret in the wine industry, with only a handful of people aware of the region's potential. Even though there are still only a dozen or so wineries, it is NSW's most exciting region. People (with or without wineries) are planting like crazy. It has sloping hillsides, a high altitude (2,600 ft/800 m) and a strong continental climate. The warm days and cool nights are the key to the zesty, ripe fruit. Even Sauvignon Blanc does well here.

Orange in New South Wales is the next Australian wine-producing region to watch.

BAROSSA VALLEY

Teutonic Barossa is a great place to grow grapes and make wine. With its not-too-wet winters and warm, dry summers, this region produces consistently reliable grapes. From the warm, sandy loam soils of the valley floor to the slightly cooler sites up in the hills, almost every style of wine is made here. Many of Australia's biggest producers have their operations here. The reds are big, generous and concentrated, while the whites are full of sunny fruit.

The Barossa Valley produces superb, fruity white wines.

MARGARET RIVER

Most winemakers in the Margaret River region go surfing every morning.
It's a magical place, where the wines benefit from the cooling effect of the sea. The region is full of with new wineries and vineyard developments. The wineries are in three main areas along the length of the Bussell Highway: namely, overlooking Geographe Bay, in Willyabrup, and southeast of Margaret River itself. New vineyards have been planted in warm Jindong, in the north, and in cooler Karridale in the south.

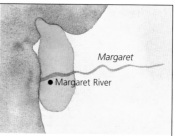

The lush green paradise of the Margaret River is home to some of Australia's top wine producers.

New Zealand

One of the smallest wine producing countries in the world, New Zealand has probably the fastest growing wine industry of them all. Not that this is very big in the general scheme of things—New Zealand produces just one percent of the world's wines. New wineries are opening up here at the rate of about 20 per year. There are two reasons for this: the domestic market can't seem to get enough, with consumption figures doubling year on year; neither can the UK—New Zealand Sauvignon Blanc is still winning British hearts. The country produces some of the world's best—and all this in the space of about 20 years.

The grapes

Chardonnay and Sauvignon Blanc dominate plantings, with Cabernet Sauvignon and Pinot Noir (much of it used in New Zealand's famous fizz) falling in behind. Other grapes on the up include Pinot Gris, Merlot and Riesling.

The regions

The North Island is warmer than the South Island, though both share a cool maritime climate. So, in general, North Island wines are a tad riper, more full-bodied and slightly softer in style, compared with those in the South Island. The undulating hills of Northland-Matakana is great red wine country, while Waiheke Island, a half-hour ferry ride from Auckland, produces trendy Bordeaux-style blends. Other regions in the north include Waikato and the Bay of Plenty, with its hallmark botrytized

Rieslings; Gisborne, which has overcome its bag-in-box reputation to produce quality whites and drinkable reds; Hawkes Bay, with its perfect climate for claret-style blends and top Chardonnays; and Wellington, with its stunning Pinot Noirs.

In the South Island, Marlborough is famous for its Sauvignon Blanc, so is Nelson, which makes other great whites, eg. fabulous lime-edged Chardonnays. Canterbury and Central Otago complete the picture, both a dab hand at Pinot Noir.

The regions

1. Northland
2. Auckland
3. Waikato
4. Bay of Plenty
5. Poverty Bay
6. Hawkes Bay
7. Wellington
8. Nelson
9. Marlborough
10. Canterbury

HAWKES BAY

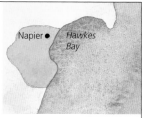

Vines used to be planted on the river flats of the Heretaunga Plain, but the fertile soils encouraged too much vigour, so many have moved to the lower slopes of the limestone hills further inland, where the grapes are riper and better balanced. Hawkes Bay's reputation rests on its serious Bordeaux-style blends. Chardonnay is also sought after – they are rich and full, but with a welcome kick of grapefruit acidity on the finish. The area is expanding fast, and a number of sub-regions have already been identified for the production of premium wines.

One of the oldest wine-producing regions in New Zealand, Hawkes Bay is also at the forefront of contemporary viniculture.

MARLBOROUGH

Who hasn't knocked back a bottle of Marlborough Sauvignon Blanc? The grape put Marlborough on the map. There's no mistaking its flavours: pungent gooseberries, green peppers, cat's pee and freshly cut grass, rounded off with a zip of lime. Its success is down to a combination of factors: the alluvial loam over deep deposits of gravel; the staggered picking (different levels of ripeness add complexity to the finished wine); better clones; leaf-plucking; a dollop of Sémillon. The legendary Cloudy Bay Vineyards act as the benchmark.

World-class Sauvignon Blanc is produced in this region.

CENTRAL OTAGO

The prize for the fastest growing region goes to isolated Central Otago. And they said you could never make wine down there. It is home to the world's most southerly vineyard and winery, the Black Ridge Vineyard. It's also the only continental climate in New Zealand and growers have adapted their viticultural practices to suit the conditions (for example, frost just when you don't want it). On the down side, consistency varies more noticeably from vintage to vintage. Chardonnay, Pinot Gris and Riesling all shine, though Pinot Noir is grabbing the most headlines.

Sauvignon Blanc, Pinot Noir, Chardonnay and Pinot Gris are all grown in the world's most southerly vineyards.

South America

South America is stealing a march on everybody else with its juicy, fruity, good-value wine. Chile and Argentina lead the way, though other South American countries, such as Brazil, Bolivia, Columbia, and even Cuba are getting in on the act.

Argentina

Let's start with the biggest wine producer in South America. How big exactly? Fifth largest in the world, that's how big. Agentina makes more wine than the whole of New Zealand—imagine that. Foreign investors are falling over themselves to grab a piece of the (still relatively cheap) action.

There's plenty of prime vineyard land for the taking, it's a winemaker's paradise.

Most of Argentina's vineyards are around Mendoza, 690 miles/1,100 km west of the country's capital Buenos Aires. The rest are spread out farther north, in San Juan, La Rioja and Salta, with some vineyards in the far south, in Patagonia's Rio Negro region. To put things into perspective, there are more than 1,000 wineries in Argentina, and 600 of them are in Mendoza.

How did they get there? The Europeans. They began moving in at the end of the nineteenth century, fencing in the wide open spaces and bringing with them vines from home—Barbera, Sangiovese, Bonarda, Torrontés, Tempranillo, and Malbec. In the early days, per capita consumption was huge—at over 100 liters. Then Coca-Cola and beer got a stranglehold. It now stands at 42 liters.

The Brits drink the rest, along with the North Americans, and a few other nationalities. UK supermarket shelves are weighed down with Argentina's cheap and cheerful varietals. Now the country is proving it can make even better wine, with a recently launched range of premium, and even superpremium wines.

Mendoza itself is 2,275 ft/700 m above sea level. Its vineyards go higher still—the highest at 4,710 ft/1,450 m in the foothills of the Andes. Most of the time the sky is

above The melting snow of the Andes irrigates the vineyards of Mendoza, in Argentina, all year round.

clear, with snowmelt from the mountains feeding the rivers through the hot summers and with the chilly night-time temperatures preserving acidity and intensity of flavor in the grapes.

It wasn't always like this. The endless, dusty desert plains stretching out below the foothills carried virtually all Argentina's vines, irrigated via a series of channels carrying water from the mountains. The result was fat grapes and plenty of them, producing quaffing wine at best. But they've learned a thing or two over the last ten years; the Argentinians saw what was being done in California and elsewhere, and the so-called "flying winemakers" have helped enormously. Now every winery seems to have a link with a top consultant or two.

left While Argentina makes most of South America's wines, other Latin countries such as Peru have produced wine for centuries.

Chile

Over the other side of the Andes is Chile. This pole bean of a country has come a long way since the early settlers and the cheery supermarket wine of the 1980s. Just like Mendoza, it's a viticultural paradise, and just like Mendoza, things are changing by the minute. Grape growers are moving off the hot valley floor to the slopes—trying out a variety here, a clone there. Soils didn't used to be such an issue as they are now.

The varietal line-up has got longer too, with nobody specializing and everybody experimenting with a whole host of varieties from the usual suspects to Sangiovese, Mourvèdre, Malbec, Tempranillo, Viognier, even an obscure Catalan variety, Garro. Clone talk is rife and the peculiarities of particular sites are discussed at length. The main regions are Aconcagua, with its two subregions of Aconcagua Valley and Casablanca Valley; The Central Valley, with its sub-regions of Maipo, Rapel, Curicó, and Maule; and The South, with up-and-coming areas such as Bío Bío.

The industry is now full with foreign winemakers—many of them women—from South Africa to New Zealand. The Chileans themselves are open to ideas from the outside, and aren't afraid to use them. The foreigners, meanwhile, like what they see in Chile, and they stay, carving out a life for themselves with a view over the Andes.

The scale of investment is huge. Instant coffee magnates, cash-rich canned fruit producers and pharmaceutical manufacturers are pouring money into Napa-style wineries. Sons and daughters of family-owned *bodegas*

The Argentinians started planting in the cooler, kinder foothills. They dug up the garlic that was growing there, kept down the yields, paid more attention in the vineyard, and started using small oak barrels—mostly French. It paid off.

The country is still very much in its experimental stages, working out what grapes should grow where, so anything goes at the moment. The star red grape, to date, is Malbec. For some reason it shines here, unlike in Bordeaux where it never gets beyond the rustic.

Specific areas have already been singled out as best for certain grapes—Tupungato for Chardonnay, for example, and Agrelo for Cabernet. There is also a growing following for the obscure Spanish grape Torrontés. Its peculiarly spicy, floral fruit goes well with aromatic foods.

(wineries), fresh from wine school, experiment with grafting more popular varieties onto their parents' unfashionable Moscatel and Sémillon vines, turning out wines that win awards thousands of miles away.

The most exciting developments have come from the Bordeaux varieties of Cabernet Sauvignon and Merlot, especially when blended. Chilean reds are booming, not least because Glasgow University, Scotland, declared their health-giving potential in a report published a couple of years ago (apparently Chilean Cabernet is packed with phenolics see page 168). There are newcomers, too, such as Syrah and Pinot Noir, which are causing a stir.

And the whites, while not yet world-class, are becoming much more diverse —Chardonnay particularly so—and not just diverse because of a varying use of oak, but because of the distinctions between soil and microclimate. The differences between, say, a Chardonnay from Bío Bío in the far south and Casablanca near the coast are fast being realized. Maybe the consumer hasn't quite caught on yet—but they will.

Sauvignon Blanc is Chile's second white hope. Chile produces around 27 percent of the world's Sauvignon Blanc, even though much of it isn't Sauvignon at all, but Sauvignonasse—not nearly such a noble variety and flabbier on the finish. True Sauvignon Blanc has more tropical notes in Chile. The Chileans were duped by the French, who sent the vines, so they are gradually replacing them.

The same thing happened with Merlot. The French sent a little known Bordeaux variety called Carmenère, but it turned out not to be the disaster first thought, and in some cases it does better than the true

Merlot clones. Viognier is yet another emerging hero, and now proudly says so on the label.

Uruguay

While Chile and Argentina are responsible for most of South America's wines, there are other countries in South America that have produced wine for centuries. Most of it isn't up to much, but there's potential in Uruguay, which now wants a slice of the export action and is gearing up to do so. It makes about the same amount of wine as New Zealand (it has a healthy domestic market) and it's not all cheap stuff. There are some soft, juicy reds coming through, made from Tannat, a grape from the Basque country, in southwest France.

below Argentina is not only the biggest wine producer in South America, it is the fifth largest producer in the world.

United States

The United States—or California, to be exact—gave us the first fresh, fruity, affordable "New World" wines, taking on the might of Europe. Wine is produced in many states, from Oregon to New York State, but California is still the biggest player.

California

If you're drinking a bottle of US wine, chances are it's Californian. Over 90 percent of US wine comes from here. The Golden State has been making wine since the middle of the nineteenth century. It's had a few stops and starts along the way —phylloxera for starters, then Prohibition, a depression and a war. But it bounced back and now makes some of the most exciting wines in the world, built on a handful of international varieties, among them Chardonnay, Merlot, Pinot Noir, and Cabernet Sauvignon. You should try a Cabernet from Napa—you will certainly see what I mean.

They call it the Pauillac of the west, with its dense, chocolate-covered black cherry, mint, and cedar fruit. Napa has the greatest concentration of vineyards and wineries in the state, and has made its name producing the nation's most prestigious wines—not to mention the most expensive. The quality doesn't always match up to the hefty price tags, but, hey, this is the richest country in the world.

When first released, the top labels are auctioned to Silicon Valley billionaires at silly prices, perpetuating their cult status. The prime vineyard spots have even sillier prices, but there's not much to go around (the Napa region is only 20 miles long).

Napa also has the largest number of Approved Viticultural Areas (AVAs), among them Stag's Leap, Howell Mountain and Oakville. AVAs are a kind of geographical identity used nationwide; if you see AVA on the label, the wine must have 85 percent of that area's grapes. If a grape is mentioned, the wine must be 75 percent from that grape. If an individual vineyard is mentioned, the wine must be 95 percent from that vineyard. A vintage must be 95 percent from that vintage.

After the flash wineries and jaw-dropping homes of Napa, neighboring Sonoma is a breath of fresh air. It has its fair share of serious wines too, but they are generally more affordable (land is about half the price), plus the wines are more approachable. It is one of California's most diverse regions, with cool coastal pockets like Russian River for Pinot Noir and hot spots like Dry Creek Valley, for sensational Zinfandel.

Zinfandel does particularly well farther south, in the Central Coast wine region of San Luis Obispo. It's the fourth largest premium coastal growing area in California

above Santa Barbara, California, is emerging as an international star in the wine world.

after Sonoma, Napa, and Monterey. The star spot for reds is around the cowboy town of Paso Robles. Farther south still is Santa Barbara County—the pundits reckon it will be the next Napa. It's grown from virtually nothing into a $100 million business in 30 years. Pinot Noir and Chardonnay grown in its Santa Ynez Valley area are stunning, and Rhône varietals have exploded here.

Other Californian wine-growing areas include Mendocino; Carneros; Santa Cruz Mountains; Lake County; Alameda; Santa Clara; San Benito, and the Sierra Foothills.

The Pacific Northwest

Okay, so Idaho is not exactly on the Pacific, but it's one of the three states that make up The Pacific Northwest Wine Coalition, formed in 1991 to promote the wines abroad. Washington and Oregon complete the picture.

Idaho has really only just started, with a couple of dozen wineries concentrated in the southwest of the state along the Snake River. Oregon has five times as many

left Oregon's Pinot Noir can and does match up to some of France's best Burgundies.

Chardonnay, which can suffer from rasping acidity and thin fruit).

The Willamette Valley is the coolest and wettest of the three designated viticultural regions, and is home to about two-thirds of Oregon's wineries. To the south lie more wine districts—the Umpqua Valley and the Rogue River region (with its subappellations of the Applegate), Illinois, and Rogue River Valleys. And there are a few vineyards in the desert climate of Eastern Oregon, Columbia Valley, and Walla Walla Valley.

wineries and it's growing still. The wine scene in Oregon once comprised a few small-scale producers, but some big operators have now moved in, pouring their cash into clone trials and site selection.

Pinot Noir is the star here. In a blind tasting back in 1980 an Oregon winemaker slipped his Pinot Noir into a line-up of top French Burgundies. It came second. The region now attracts many foreign investors on a quest for the best Pinot.

Oregon is also becoming known for other varietals, especially Pinot Gris, which is fast ousting easy-selling Chardonnay (Oregon is too wet, some say, for

While Oregon sits glumly through the steady rain, which falls between November and April, Washington State covets water for its tumbleweed-choked vineyards. There are shifts of as much as 40–50°F between day and nighttime temperatures, with summer highs hitting 100°F, and bone-chilling winters that can get to 20 degrees below. It's amazing that fine wine grapes can survive these hardships, but the plants toughen up soon enough, the fruit's intensity due in part to the extra

below The majority of Oregon's wineries are to be found in the Willamette Valley.

hours of sunshine it gets up here. Growers are gradually moving their vineyards off the hot valley floors to the more protective hills, with the best sites bagged by the more pioneering among them, their fruit fought over by the region's top wineries.

There are four main appellations and six further subappellations, each with its own set of conditions. The biggest is Columbia Valley, much smaller is Yakima Valley, then there's Walla Walla, and Puget Sound. Merlot, in particular, does well here, but Syrah is the grape on everybody's lips. It packs a punch and the state was made for it. There are also fine whites made from Chardonnay, Riesling, Sémillon, and Sauvignon Blanc.

New York State

The New York State wine industry is going through a bit of boom. The area, to the east of the Big Apple, has actually been making wine for decades. It was even once America's second largest producer of wine, although now it falls behind all the above. But, as with many up-and-coming wine regions, money has been spent on the latest technology, and more thought has gone into grape selection. The Finger Lakes produce most of the state's wines, overlooking a series of lakes—indeed, it's the lakes that make wine-grape-growing possible,

protecting the vines against hazardous frosts and moderating the climate in the winter months. There is some decent Chardonnay and Riesling, though grapes like Cabernet Sauvignon and Merlot are grown here too. Sparkling wines and ice wines are also specialities.

The wineries on Long Island are as slick-looking as the houses. It's the warmest and mildest growing region in the state, so grapes like Cabernet Sauvignon have a good run. It's divided into two AVAs: The Hamptons and North Fork. Best of the red varieties are Merlot and Cabernet Franc, while Sauvignon Blanc is the best white grape in the state.

There are two further New York State wine regions, Lake Erie and Hudson River.

Other states

Of the remaining states of America, 36 of them (Hawaii included) produce wines. There are the odd bright stars in New Mexico, Maryland, Virginia, and Arizona, but as yet, there's not much to write home about here.

above The vineyards of North Fork, New York State, produce a smaller quantity of wine, but the quality is one to watch.

Canada

Canada's wines have had a bit of rough ride with the British press in the past. "The only thing worth drinking is the Icewine," they sniped. The ice wine is truly delicious, made mainly from Riesling grapes picked (at some risk to the fingers) in the depths of winter and turned into the sweetest-tasting nectar. But Canada is on the cusp of producing great table wines. It has even got its first wine research and teaching center, at Brock University, in Ontario. Sure, it's not there yet—it has still got some experimenting to do (what grapes grow best where and all that kind of stuff), but the investment is there, and so is the know-how. Even Burgundy producers are shelling out for new vineyards in joint venture agreements—so it must be okay.

The grapes

Anything goes. There's Chardonnay; Gamay; Gewürztraminer; Cabernet Franc; Merlot; Riesling; Pinot Blanc; Pinot Noir; Viognier; Chenin Blanc; Ehrenfelser (a Riesling and Sylvaner cross); Maréchal Foch (a hardy, early-ripening French hybrid, producing fruity, light-bodied wines); Baco Noir (smoky bacon and rich, dark fruit); and Vidal (a thick-skinned French hybrid that does well in Icewine).

The regions

Though four of Canada's ten provinces are suitable for growing vines, the majority of vineyards are in just two provinces: the Niagara Peninsula in Ontario and the Okanagan Valley in British Columbia.

Okanagan Valley

Vancouver Island

Montreal • Quebec

Toronto • Niagara District

Pelee Island

left The vision of enthusiastic wine growers some 30 years ago is now being realized in the idyllic Okanagan Valley.

to go around.

Pickers compete with hungry bears for grapes in British Columbia—they are not an unusual sight at harvest time. Virtually all the vineyards here are in the Okanagan Valley, with the crystal-clear lake as its centerpiece. It's a stunning spot, with two clearly defined parts: the cooler north of the valley, where aromatic whites such as Pinot Gris and Riesling do well, and the hot, arid south, with its sagey Cabernets and Merlots. Merlot, in fact, is Canada's most successful variety to date. The wine scene only started here in the 1970s, but thanks to a bunch of enthusiastic producers, the potential is about to be realized.

A word of advice: if you ever want to explore both, go to British Columbia second—the scenery will blow your mind and just accentuate the flatness of the first. Ontario does have its own charms, though. The lakes for one—you can't get away from the water. It has a moderating influence on the climate. It can get rather hot and humid in the summer, but on paper, the average monthly temperatures compare to many of the world's fine wine-producing hot spots.

Ontario produces 75 percent of Canada's wines, in many different styles, though most of it is white. Most of the vineyards are on the Niagara Peninsula.

The talk here is of "benches"—areas with different soils under a high ridge called the Niagara Escarpment. Each bench will give different characteristics to the finished wine. Riesling is particularly good. In the right hands, the wines are sumptuous, though the current trend away from the grape means that, sadly, there isn't enough

The quality

Check that there is a VQA (Vintners' Quality Alliance) seal on the bottle. The VQA charter sets the regulations and makes sure producers keep to them. There are two quality levels. First there is Provincial Designation, where the wines must be made from one or more *Vitis vinifera* or *vinifera* hybrid grapes (from an approved list), grown within the designated province. If the wine is a varietal, then it must contain 85 percent of that variety. Next comes Geographic Designation, which is a tougher regulation, based on Designated Viticultural Areas (DVAs), whereby a minimum of 85 percent of the grapes must come from

right Riesling grapes are harvested for icewine in the snowy, winter landscape of St Catherine's, Ontario.

Other Countries

This section is a real eye-opener. Bet you didn't know that wine is made in Japan, or India, or China. Odd spots in Europe are easier to grasp—and who knows, Greece could be the next big thing in wine production.

left Mountains form a dramatic back-drop to the snow-covered vineyards of Valais, Switzerland's main wine-producing area.

recognizable, varieties include Gamay, Pinot Noir, and Merlot. Most of the vineyards are in the French-speaking cantons, with Valais grabbing the lion's share.

Switzerland

Sorry, Switzerland, to stick you in "Other Countries," but it's because of your lack of prominence on the shelves. Not that you aren't trying to address this—you are—but as yet, your average wine drinker has so many other countries to tackle first.

Switzerland is trying its hardest to make an impact outside the country. It has no problem selling its wine to the natives, but by the time you've whacked on duty and all the rest, these wines are rather pricey once they are exported.

There's not much of it around either. Chasselas is the most widely planted variety, and while it doesn't exactly excite elsewhere, it can make really interesting whites in Switzerland. The country has other unusual grapes, too, including Petite Arvine, Amigne, and Humagne Blanc. Other, more

Luxembourg

Luxembourg, curiously, has a thriving little wine industry, with most of its Germanic varieties planted along the banks of the Mosel River. But, sadly, that's just about all the space it deserves, as the wines rarely make it outside the country, and, anyway, there isn't much to get excited about.

Moldova and Montenegro

Moldova and Montenegro make wine too, though you won't see them. They have a long way to go, and they haven't quite grasped the concept of marketing, but the potential in Montenegro, at least, is there.

Greece

It's the same story—the wines are way down the wine-drinkers' priority list. Greece is behind almost every European country in terms of wine quality, modernization, and investment. Though, once again, things are changing. Greek wine, and not just Retsina, has finally reached wine stores.

There are wines from individual estates, made from interesting, indigenous varieties with hard-to-pronounce names, such as Xynomavro, Agiorgitiko, and Moscophilero. Thankfully, Greek producers, while also growing international grapes, are keen to keep up with their native grapes.

Cyprus

Think of Cyprus and fortified wine springs to mind. But Cyprus is making some drinkable light reds. New plantings of Grenache and Carignan thrive alongside native varietals, such as Mavro, Promara, and Maratheftico. There's new investment, and better vineyard management.

Croatia and Macedonia

Before we leave this part of the world, Croatia and Macedonia should get a brief mention—brief, because while it has suitable wine country, the social and political climate is holding things back somewhat, so don't expect to see any of their wines in a shop near you now.

Turkey

Turkey deserves a mention too, though only in passing, because nothing of any interest leaves its shores, or indeed, stays there. What little wine there is (made mostly for tourists) is old-fashioned and comprises thin, alcoholic reds and oxidized whites.

India

Heading east—a lot farther east—is India. Yes, India has a burgeoning wine industry. The French, Americans, Australians et al are sniffing out investment opportunities as the country's appetite for wine grows. Some foreign investors are there already, with

internationally renowned wine consultants doing their bit with established wineries. Grapes such as Ugni Blanc, Chardonnay, Colombard, and Pinot Blanc are planted at high altitudes to make passable bubbly and whites. Reds are following, from Cabernet Sauvignon to Pinot Noir.

China

China is another one full of surprises. Amazingly, it produces the same amount of wine as Chile, but we just don't get to hear about it because its vast population is drinking most of it themselves. Once again, the country is attracting a lot of interest from foreign investors. The Shandong Peninsula is where most of the action is, and Western growers are giving the locals a helping hand. There's already some decent Chardonnay, plus wine made from German and even Russian grape varieties.

Japan

Japan has been growing grapes since time began; it's just that they would rather eat the fruit than make it into wine. The most popular grape is Koshu, and there are a handful of European varieties, but most of the country and climate are unsuitable for making wines.

below Wine production in China has already reached healthy levels and looks set for a promising future.

wine
science

Now, attention please, here comes the technical stuff. Actually,

the basics are quite straightforward. You'll never be able to look

at another vineyard again without running your fingers through

the soil, or pondering over the way a vine is pruned. You might

even eventually be able to say with some authority, "Those yields

look a bit too high." And, believe it or not, you'll also fall in love

with a nasty-looking fungus. You'll view "old-fashioned" drinks

such as sherry and Madeira in a totally new light. And then here

comes the best bit—proof positive that a little wine each day is

actually good for your health. Enjoy.

Location, Location, and Location

It is always the winemaker who takes the credit for a delicious bottle of wine these days. It's true that his or her job is very important: a winemaker can steer even a bad harvest towards a decent glug with technology such that it is. But nothing the winemaker does influences the taste quite so much as the raw materials and the conditions in which they are grown.

You have already been introduced to the different grape varieties, which, of course, influence the flavor hugely. But how and where they are grown accounts for much of the individuality of a wine. Conditions may repeat themselves, sure, but often a particular area's geology and climate are unique.

You can't grow wine vines in just any old place (though Japan, and even Thailand, are having a go). Ideally, winters should be cold —cold enough to let the vine shut down to conserve energy until the spring. In the spring, when the vine begins to flower, it needs sun, right through to harvest if possible, with just a measure of summer rainfall followed by a gentle, drying breeze and a long, dry fall.

The wine-producing regions of the world lie in two sharply defined bands around the globe: the moderate, temperate zones that lie between 50° and 30° in the northern hemisphere and 30° and 50° in the southern hemisphere.

The rule used to be that the cooler areas farthest away from the equator made the finest wine, while the hotter vineyard areas

left The Languedoc is situated almost in the center of the moderate temperate zone of the northern hemisphere.

may not reach full ripeness—even with that south-facing slope. To make wine, there must be enough sugar in the grape to be converted, by yeast, into alcohol. And the sun puts the sugar content there.

Uncertain weather, particularly frost or hail, during vine flowering in late spring can also reek havoc by affecting the number of flowers that are fertilized—and therefore the number of grapes.

Too much sun? Then irrigate; many New World vineyards wouldn't exist without irrigation. However, irrigation is still viewed with suspicion by many Europeans who have quite enough water, thank you. True, irrigation is not monitored with the kind of regulations that the winemakers would like (they complain there are too many high-yields from too liberal use of irrigation), but there are systems in place that are sophisticated enough to read the exacting needs of the soil and the grape.

produced high-yield wines of quaffing quality. But now many winemakers in hot countries are doing their best to pick earlier and manage the grapevines better, plus numerous other clever tricks, to mimic the condition of cooler climates.

The nearer the equator you get, the more difficult it is to produce quality wine. Tropical rains result in nasty fungal diseases (in fact, too much rain anywhere encourages diseases) and because there's no winter, the vine doesn't get a chance to rest, so just keeps on producing barely ripe fruit, up to three crops a year, in "seasons" artificially manipulated by pruning and irrigation.

But it rains a lot in cooler climates, and that's not good for the grapes either. The sun can indeed be elusive in cooler climate areas, so the sunniest spots are sought. The best in the northern hemisphere are the south-facing slopes, which from dawn until dusk soak up all the rays going.

The sun—or rather lack of it—is the main problem for vine-growers in cool climates because in some years the grapes

below Planting vineyards on a south-facing slope (in the northern hemisphere) makes sure of maximum exposure to the sun's rays.

Getting Down to Earth

above Vineyards extend down the slope beneath the towering outcrop of the landmark Rock of Solutré in the Mâconnais.

So you've got the perfect vineyard site, but the way in which you select and plant your vines will dictate the quality of your fruit. The ideal spot is halfway up a hillside. Vines planted on the flat get less sunshine, are badly drained and are prone to frost. The lowest part of the hill may suffer from damp—especially if there is a river nearby. Vines halfway up get the most sunshine and the best drainage. Too high, and the cooler temperature in the higher altitude may affect the grapes' chances of ripening. Forget the top—it's too cool, too windy and, if tree-clad, not sunny enough.

Different soils suit different vines. The soil—or rather the drainage of the soil

—will affect the taste of the wine. Well-drained soil is warm. Soggy soil is cold. It's the temperature of the soil—even more than the air—that kick-starts a vine into budding. That's not to say that well-drained soil is always better than a thick wet, clay soil. Well-drained soils can be prone to frosts or may reflect too much heat onto the grapes. A cold clay soil can hold back early-ripening vines like Merlot, and give the wine more structure.

How does the soil affect the taste of the grapes? Take Chardonnay, for example. Grown in Chablis, on limestone soils, the wine will have a flinty, mineral quality. But Chardonnay grown in California's clay soils will taste much heavier.

How many soil types are there? There are many, but there are four key types to

right Slate soils such as that found in Mosel, Germany, retain heat well, compensating for any lack of sun.

remember. Let's start with chalk. It's got good drainage and forces the vines to work harder. Not all vine varieties like alkaline soils—those that do best on chalky hillsides produce characterful white wines, such as Chardonnay. The key point to remember with grapes grown on chalky—limestone—soil is their acidity. Think Champagne, Chablis, and Sancerre.

Next up is granite. The stones act as reflectors, bouncing the heat from the sun back on to the grapes, giving big, alcohol-high reds like Châteauneuf-du-Pape.

Then there's gravelly soil. Many vineyards are positioned on the sides of river valleys. Vines do best in poor, well-drained soils. Their roots plunge deep to find nutrients. Cabernet Sauvignon loves this kind of soil (think Graves, the Bordeaux appellation; it means "gravel"). Though it does depend what it's mixed with: if the gravel is sitting over clay, the wine will have less acidity than if it is sitting on limestone.

Finally, slate. These soils are packed with minerals, which suit some vines perfectly and, in regions like the Mosel in Germany,

are good at retaining heat, which compensates for any lack of sun.

Move a hectare or two to the left or right in a wine region, and the story may change, sometimes even dramatically. Through the ages, certain patches of land have produced better wine than their immediate neighbors—no matter how much money is thrown at the inferior site. You just have to look at Bordeaux—the names of the great first growth clarets have been revered since the nineteenth century. Or Burgundy, with its complicated, hierarchical patchwork of different vineyards and appellations. This is summed up neatly by *terroir*, which is France's elegant word for the combination of soil, the lie of the land, and the climate.

BUG BOX

Phylloxera. Say that word to a wine-grape-grower and he'll shudder. It's a tiny louse that loves nothing more than munching through a vinifera vine root—it'll destroy a vineyard. At the end of the last century, it destroyed most French vineyards, then went on to munch its way through vines in the rest of the wine-producing world. Eventually a solution was found. By grafting vinifera vines on to American rootstock, the vulnerable bits of the plant became resistant to it. Since then, nurseries the world over have worked on breeding phylloxera-resistant rootstocks. It does pop up again from time to time, notably in Northern California in the 1990s, and a costly replanting program is still under way.

Plant and Grow

So you've prepared your vineyard. You know the soil type. You've studied the climate. You know which vines (and which clones) you will plant on to what phylloxera-resistant rootstock (see page 151). But how closely do you plant the vines? How will you prune them? How will you train them? These are just a couple of the questions that face the wine-grape-grower.

For many Old World vine-growers, these decisions have already been made—though that's not to say there isn't room for improvement. The current craze for wines that are ready to drink now means that many changes are taking place in vineyards across the Old World. Better canopy management, for example, means riper grapes, and riper grapes mean more fruit-driven wines. Combine this with, say, a de-stemming machine in the winery and you've got wines that are ready to drink within two years of harvest—as opposed to

below Choosing how to grow vines means juggling many factors—these Sauvignon Blanc grapes are showing signs of sunburn.

the five years we were expected to wait in the past.

Let's start with vine density. Wet northern France, for example, can achieve a vine density of up to 10,000 vines per hectare, while the arid plains in Spain, where the vines need to work a larger area of soil to get moisture, manage about 1,400 plants per hectare.

The spacing between the rows differs from Old World to New World, too. The Old World vineyards have room enough for a person (or, until recently, a horse) to move about between the vines. If machines are used, then they are adapted to work the relatively low, neat rows. Many New World vineyards were designed for machine picking right from the start, so the rows can be as much as 10 ft/3 m apart.

The direction you decide to plant the vines—from north to south, east to west —is also a matter for deliberation, taking in the vagaries of the climate: elements like wind, sun, and soil erosion.

There are also many different thoughts on vine-training. One old-fashioned way is the bush vine: vines grow unsupported like wild bushes. The most popular way to train is to run the vine along wires. It controls the vigor—the leaf count—of the vine, which in turn prevents the spread of diseases. Training also allows good air circulation (so that the grapes won't rot) and generally works well with the elements. There are innumerable methods: among those encountered are single and double guyot, Geneva double curtain, and gobelet.

Canopy management is another phrase you might hear. This "sculpts" the vine, exposing the grapes when high rainfall encourages greater vigor, which hides the grapes from the sun's precious ripening rays. How much and when you prune the vine will affect the plant's yield.

Old vines. That's another thing you'll see on labels. A vine is ready to crop commercially in its third year, then keeps on producing steadily until it's about 20 years old. After this, the quantity starts to decline —but not necessarily the quality. In fact, the quality of the grapes often increases, which is why you see so much boasting of "old

above Old World vineyards, such as this one in Basilicata, Italy, were traditionally planted in rows with sufficient space for people to move between them, whereas the rows in many New World vineyards are much wider apart as they were designed for machine picking.

vines" on wine labels these days (though this can mean anything from 10 to 100 years).

What the vine-grower is aiming for is grapes with grape sugars (produced from sunlight and water by the photosynthesis that makes all plants grow) that are balanced by a suitable level of acidity. As the sugar levels increase, so too do all those yummy flavors.

Gathering the Harvest

It's thirsty work doing a harvest. And also backbreaking, in fact, because pickers stoop to part the leaves and snip away at the best-looking bunches. But what has happened to the vine, exactly, before this day?

Let's start in winter. It looks like there's no sign of life—blackened stumps jutting out of the hard earth, with naked, spindly branches. The vines have shut down. They're conserving all their energy until the spring. They enjoy the rest. The rigor of carrying and ripening a crop is exhausting stuff. In really cold climates—like Canada and sometimes in Germany and Austria—grapes are left on the vine after harvest to gather more sugar and eventually freeze on the vine, resulting in a sweet wine of staggering concentration called Eiswein/Icewine (see sweet wines, page 32).

Pruning is just about the only thing going on in a vineyard in winter. It's important to prune at this stage, particularly in cooler climates—because it is the main way (along with high-density planting) that a grape-grower can plan out his yields for the year, determining, most importantly, the number of bunches each vine is to produce.

What are *yields*? The quantity of wine produced from grapes is measured in Europe as hectoliters of wine per hectare of vineyard. In the United States, it's measured as tons of grapes per acre. The figures are also affected by the characteristics of the grape, what sort of wine is being made, and how hard the grapes are pressed.

In quality wine production, low yields are generally accepted as standard—especially in cool climates.

leaving the remainder to ripen better. The canopy—the leaves—may be trimmed back too, to allow the sun's rays in to ripen the fruit further. Birds get interested at this point, so antibird netting may be necessary.

Acidity levels will decrease as time goes on, and the grapes will start to soften and change color—this is known as *veraison*. Then the pace picks up. A smattering of summer rain is good here to protect against the drying effects of the sun. For those who don't have that luxury, irrigation is essential.

The grape ripens, and fall is in the air. Suddenly it's harvest time. The grower has to decide when it's right to pick. Does he risk the weather and let his grapes stay for another few days on the vine to up the sugar levels? Or should he start picking immediately; maybe that forecast isn't so good after all.

The big moment has arrived. The picking begins. The grapes are carefully transported to the winery to be pressed and transformed into wine.

below Traditional wicker baskets display a fine crop of Pinot Noir grapes—but you need powerful biceps to carry them.

It's spring and tiny green shoots emerge from the buds left on the vine after winter pruning. Frost is the big danger here. Growers use all kinds of methods to combat it: from crude heaters placed at the end of each row of vines to—a bit excessive this—helicopters hovering over the top of the vines to warm up the air. Vines are damaged below 23°F/-5°C. As spring advances, pests become a problem too.

Then it's flower time. This lasts for a week or two, up to 12 weeks after the first buds appear. Some are fertilized to become berries, or grapes. The weather, once again, has an effect on the size of the crop.

During summer, the sun does its stuff transforming the hard, green pellets to fat, juicy fruit. If there are too many grapes, there's a green harvest (or crop thinning), where some bunches are cut off by hand,

left Hand picking grapes is labor intensive and can be backbreaking work.

How White Wine is Made

above Separated from the stalks, grapes emerge from a machine that de-stems and crushes them.

Did you know that you could make white wine from red grapes? It's true. Though not that frequent. The Champagne region does it all the time, with Pinot Noir and Pinot Meunier. In fact, white wine can be made from any color grape, so long as there is no skin contact or maceration with dark-skinned grapes.

So you've got your white grapes. You've also got lots of lovely, spotless stainless steel equipment—cleanliness is the buzz word in white-wine making. Red, too, of course, but particularly so when making white wine. Control is the name of the game. You don't want too much oxygen or unwanted bacteria.

A lot of the harvesting and crushing is done early in the day—especially in hot climates. The main aim is to get the juice out of the grapes as quickly as possible, to ferment that juice, then bottle the wine —or barrel it in oak to pick up more flavours—but retaining as much of the grape's delicious flavors as possible. There you have it—the art of white wine making in a nutshell.

The winemaking process

The grapes are picked and sorted—any rotten ones are discarded. They are then taken to the winery as fast as possible, to avoid being crushed by their own weight and oxidized.

If you're going for a lighter, unwooded style of dry white wine, the grapes are crushed and separated from their stalks by a de-stemmer or crusher. Sulfur dioxide is added to prevent the juice oxidizing and spoiling. It helps kill bacteria and any unwanted wild yeasts. You sometimes get a whiff of burnt matches when you open a bottle of unwooded white or sweet wine. That's the sulfur. But once you've exposed the wine to some air the smell soon goes.

The crushed grapes are then pressed, forcing the juice out but leaving the skins. The juice is pumped into a cold, stainless steel tank to settle. Yeast is added. That's another hot topic: which yeast? In the old days, winemakers relied on the local "wild" yeasts, which can take time to work their magic, but today's winemakers—especially in new wine regions—mostly use cultured yeasts, which tend to be more predictable. Of course, there are plenty of mavericks who think wild is best, arguing that you get more complexity in a wine.

Then fermentation begins. This can be fast, slow, warm or cool. The norm for whites is 50–77°F (10–25°C).

Go into a modern winery now and you'll see the space-age control panels that monitor and control the temperature of each vat with the flick of a switch. The winemaker can dictate the flavors and character of a wine by controlling the fermentation temperatures—generally, the cooler the fermentation, the fruitier the wine. And whites, which depend on primary fruit aromas and have no need to encourage extraction, are almost always fermented cooler than most reds.

A few days later, fermentation is finished. The new wine is then pumped off its lees (dead yeast cells and other gunk that has settled at the bottom of the tank) into another tank. The temperature is brought down again, then a clarifying agent, such as egg whites, is added to gather up any other gunk that is floating around in there: this process is called fining. Don't worry—the egg doesn't stay in the wine, it is merely there to attract the solids.

If the sun was lacking and so the grape sugars are rather low, sugar may be added to increase the alcohol level: this is called *chaptalization*. If there's not enough acidity, tartaric or citric acid can be added to correct the balance. But you can't do both chaptalization *and* acidification.

The wine is then filtered and bottled.

right Modern wineries are equipped with space-age stainless steel tanks and complex control panels.

Full-bodied white wine

To make full-bodied, wooded dry white wine, the rules are followed up until the fermentation stage. But then before fermentation has finished, the wine is pumped into oak barrels. The new wine stays there for around six to eight months to absorb the oaky vanilla flavors, fattening out the fruit, adding longevity-bearing tannin and giving it some complexity. This isn't suitable for all white grapes—but Chardonnay, for example, loves oak.

After that, the wine is pumped into a tank, as before, then stabilized, fined (see page 172), filtered, and bottled.

Talking of oak: the type and size of the oak barrel that the winemaker chooses will have an enormous influence on the flavor of the wine. New barrels give the wine a more oaky flavor than old barrels. Smaller barrels give the wine a more oaky flavor than big barrels. American oak gives the wine a more obvious oak flavor than French barrels. Oak from one forest differs from another. It goes on. See the section on oak in How Red Wines are Made (pages 160–161).

But oak barrels cost. And there are plenty of cheaper wooded whites around that have never seen an oak barrel. Enter the oak chip or stave. Add a bag of oak chips, or staves, to a stainless steel tank of fermenting dry white wine and you get instant oak flavoring. This is not particularly complex, because the wine doesn't get all the advantages of barrel aging, but for those who like a piece of buttered toast with their white, this is an economical alternative.

Making the wine special

Just as a top chef has his own twist on a classic recipe, so the winemaker has his own way of doing things. The individuality of a wine is down to the winemaker's skill and intuition. The temperature of fermentation —and the length of time it is allowed to carry on—is a key factor in the wine's individual character. As is the choice of barrels—age and size—or stainless steel tanks and the strain of yeast used.

Then there is malolactic fermentation— or "malo," as it's known to its buddies—to contend with. Virtually all red wines, and

an increasing number of whites (mostly wooded), undergo this second, "softening" fermentation, where the crisp, hard malic acid is converted by bacteria to much softer, lactic acid. It can happen all on its own, but most winemakers induce it, either by keeping the new wine at relatively high temperatures, and/or by deliberately introducing the lactic bacteria. As well as making the wine more stable, it makes it taste softer, fuller, and more complex. Overdo it, and you end up with a buttery mess. The winemaker might just want to mix in a small amount of malo, to soften out a crisp, dry wine. Again, oak-fermented and aged Chardonnay is often put through malolactic fermentation, and this gives the wine its characteristic creamy, butteriness.

And finally there's the lees. Remember, the gunky bits that sink to the bottom? A winemaker can add complexity to his wine by stirring up the lees every week or so. It encourages extra layers of flavor from the lees themselves. The lees are usually racked off for lighter styles of wine, but if he's going for something bigger, and more buttery, that is matured in the barrel, then he might want to keep the wine in contact with its lees a little longer. Red wines almost always sit on their lees.

And there you have it.

below Cleanliness remains a priority through the process to the final bottling of the wine.

How Red Wine is Made

One of the most difficult jobs in red-wine making is shoveling the spent skins out of the vat when the wine is finished fermenting. You pity those poor cellar rats (affectionate term for a winery worker) covered from head to toe in remnants of juice and skin as they scrape out the bottom. Making red wine is, without a doubt, harder than making white wine.

What's the big difference? Skin, in a word. If you were just to press the grapes, leaving the skins behind, you would get white wine. But people don't—the point is the skins. Ferment the juice together with the skins of red grapes and the color and flavor emerge. Or that's the theory. The skins can be difficult sometimes—so this is where the skills of the expert wine-maker come in.

Let's start at the crusher, loaded up with freshly picked bunches of red grapes, where it just breaks the skins. Depending on what style of wine is being made, and the amount of tannin needed, the stalks may or may not be dumped at this stage. The stalks can add nasty flavors and too much astringency, if care is not taken.

From here, the grapes go straight into the fermentation vats—skins and all. Yeast (wild or cultured) is added. Fermentation can take four weeks or longer to complete. Red wine is fermented at a higher temperature (ranging from 64–95°F/ 18–35°C) than white. The higher the temperature, the more color and tannin is extracted. Cooler wine regions sometimes need the higher temperatures to encourage

above For the unusual Recioto della Valpolicalla Amarone, the grapes are allowed to dry and shrivel before fermentation.

color, flavor, and tannin. There are, of course, exceptions. Wines such as Beaujolais are fermented using carbonic maceration. The whole berries are bathed in carbon dioxide. A yeast-free fermentation takes place inside each berry. Result: bright raspberry red fruit with soft, fruity flavors and a distinctive smell of pear-drops, for drinking young. There are also a number of top quality red wine producers (Pinot Noir fanatics particularly) who tip whole bunches, stalks and all, into open fermentation vats —open, to allow the "cap" (the layer of grape solids that floats on the top) to be broken up. In a quest for structure and complexity they either pump the juice over the cap, punching it down once or twice a day (more back-breaking stuff), or sub-merge the cap completely.

Fermentation over, the new purple wine is separated from its skins (including the last solid bits at the bottom, which are

left Open fermentation vats have their fanatical fans, but it is backbreaking work for the winemaker.

barrels from all over the world, including Hungary and Georgia. Although only a fraction of the world's wine ends up in barrels (much of it is made in cheaper stainless steel tanks), most of the world's best wines are aged in oak barrels.

But why oak? Other woods, such as pine, chestnut, and redwood, have been used for larger wine vats, but oak is the best for smaller barrels (about 225 liters) because it is strong and water-tight, yet supple, with a not entirely understood affinity with wine.

Then there's the question of which forest? Ideally, the wood should be from trees 80–100 years old. Coopers distinguish between wine-friendly, tight-grained oaks from slow-growing, densely planted forests, and the more porous, wide-grained oaks favored by brandy producers. The most revered oaks for winemaking come from central France—Allier and Nevers in the upper Loire, or from the Vosges hills west of Alsace. Look out for the stamp on the barrel the next time you visit a winery.

pressed with varying degrees of strength) and pumped into barrels. However, many European producers deliberately leave the new wine in the fermentation vat for a couple of days to a few weeks (depending on how much extract the winemaker wants) after fermentation has finished to squeeze a bit more color from the skins. Try it in a warmer climate and things can get a little too tannic, so some producers even separate the juice from the skins before fermentation is over, finishing it off in the barrel—called barrel fermentation. This is big in Australia, for example, and results in wines with a sweet, toasty nose.

The importance of oak

Enter oak—the second most important ingredient in winemaking after the grape itself. Producers love to show off their barrels; the oak adds gravitas and value to their wines. It is widely acknowledged to be the magic ingredient in winemaking because wood can impart flavor, color, and tannin. The barrels cost, too, with certain coopers (the barrelmakers) and woods revered above others.

There's a pecking order. French oak barrels have the best reputation and the highest price tag, but you can get oak

below The choice of oak for making the barrels—French is thought to be the best—is a crucial part of the winemaking process.

There's much talk, too, about American oak—the country is the biggest commercial grower of oak. It is much more powerful than French oak and imparts a sweet vanilla flavor to wine. It is mainly used for red wines in the Americas, Spain (it has a tradition of importing American barrels), and Australia, but it works well with warm climate Chardonnays too.

Then we get on to the level of toasting inside the barrels—another flavor enhancer in wine. If the cooper gives the wood a light toast, the barrel is more likely to give off more oak flavor and tannins to a wine than a barrel with a medium toast. Heavily toasted barrels can give their own kind of caramelized flavor to a wine.

The newer the barrel, the more oak flavor and tannin it gives to a wine. Brand new barrels are the most highly prized. But by the third time around, the barrel has almost no flavor left to give.

Red wine spends more time in oak than white—usually nine to eighteen months, depending on how much body and structure the winemaker is going for. Light, quaffing reds for immediate consumption are, of course, the exception here, and are invariably left in stainless steel.

How rosé wines are made

In case you're wondering, rosés, or pink wines, are made just like white wines, except that the juice is lightly tinted from a short contact with red skins before fermentation. Another way of making pink wine is to bleed off some of the juice in a vat of crushed red grapes soon after fermentation has started, or at a basic level you could just add a splash of red wine to some white wine for a homemade solution.

above In open fermentation vats, the juice is pumped over the "cap" once or twice a day.

The art of blending, fining, and filtering

Red (and white) wines are almost always blended. It could be a blend of different vineyards, or even different clones of the same grape in the same vineyard; it could be a blend of two tanks of the same wine, but made in different ways; it could be a blend of different grape varieties: Chardonnay and Sémillon or Cabernet Sauvignon, Merlot, and Malbec. This is how the winemaker is really able to control the style of wine.

Then it's just a matter of fining and filtering (or not) before bottling. Fining and filtering helps to stabilize the wine and protect against unwanted bacteria, as well as getting rid of the gunky bits that settle in the bottom of a bottle. But some winemakers think that it strips the wine of its character and so don't bother.

Adding a Bit of Sparkle

left Krug is the only Champagne house to continue using barrel fermentation for its base wine production.

Bubbly is made in every wine-producing country in the world. And there are ways, and ways, of making it.

The classic method

The classic—and best—way is called Méthode Traditionelle: used for Champagne, Cava, Crémant, Blanquette de Limoux, good New World bubblies, Italian Metodo Classico, and some German Sekt. Blend your base wines (whole bunches gently pressed and fermented with yeast to make an unwooded dry white wine, which is then blended with other base wines, some made from the year or two before, until you get the right balance of acidity, length and complexity) with a little yeast and sugar. Then bottle it, stack it on its side in a cool cellar and wait for the secondary fermentation—at least 18 months.

The bottles are then put, neck first, into specially designed racks, called *pupitres*. Enter the riddler (or *remueur*, in French). The riddler rotates the bottles gradually,

over about a month or so, to shake down the sediment (the *lees*) so that it rests on the cork. There are machines now that do this (called *giropalettes*), but a few Champagne houses prefer to carry on doing things the old-fashioned way.

The necks of the bottles are then chilled, freezing the sediment into a solid plug. When the corks are removed, the frozen plug pops out, and the wine is topped up with more of the same wine and a little liquid sugar (called the *dosage*), before being corked, tied down with wire and left for a few months to settle, before releasing on to the market.

The transfer method

This is the next best way after Méthode Traditionelle: used by some New World fizz. The secondary fermentation takes place in the bottle and the wine is transferred under pressure to tanks for dosage, filtering, and re-bottling.

The tank method

The tank method (sometimes known as *cuvée close*, or *Charmat*, after the bloke who invented it) is the most common method and is used for quick, cheap and easy French and Spanish fizz, most German Sekt, and most Asti Spumante. The base wine is run into huge stainless steel tanks where secondary fermentation takes place at a controlled temperature, followed by dosage, filtering, and bottling.

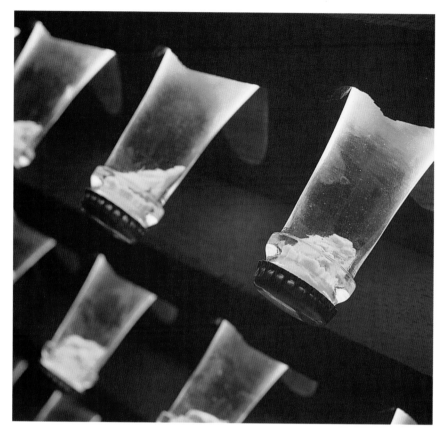

Carbonation

Carbonation is the same as for fizzy soft drinks. A tank of base wine is injected with carbon dioxide and bottled under pressure. This is the crudest method, and it results in a dramatic, but short-lived, explosion of bubbles.

The Champagne effect

Why is Méthode Traditionelle the best? Simply because it brings out the flavors of the grapes best. You can use any grapes, though many producers stick to the same mix as those used in Champagne: Chardonnay, Pinot Noir, and Pinot Meunier. The best base wines for making bubbly are generally those with high acidity and little character, so those grown in cool climates are best.

Although they are usually blended, Chardonnay and Pinot Noir are sometimes

above The sediment collects in the neck of the bottles as they are gradually rotated in the pupitres.

made into sparkling wines on their own: 100 percent Chardonnay is known as *blanc de blancs*; 100 percent Pinot Noir is called *blanc de noirs*.

The blend of the base wine is the important thing with the best bubbly: it could combine 40 different still wines. It requires an enormous amount of experience to predict what those wines will do to the finished product.

Why does Champagne cost so much? Well, because the French are clever. Generations of Champagne producers have convinced us that fizz is somehow more special than table wine—although it has to be said that making Champagne does require much more money, time, and effort.

How Sweet Wine is Made

Some of the world's best wine is sweet wine. Just think of Château d'Yquem (and think is probably the closest you'll get, because it is highly prized and highly priced). But offer a glass of sweet wine, and the response, invariably, is negative. The lack of enthusiasm is more to do with past experiences: a lot of sweet wine is totally undrinkable. Far too many sweet wines lack sufficient acidity to balance the residual sugar. Sulfur dioxide has played a part in its downfall too—winemakers used to (and some still do) add vast quantities of it to ward off any unwanted yeast activity, with throat-tickling results. No, really good sweet wine should be well balanced, made from grapes picked late, with all the natural sweetness of really ripe fruit.

The best

Rot is vital—noble rot, to be exact. Or *Botrytis cinerea* to give it its proper name. In the right kind of weather, the airborne fungus dries out the ripe grapes, substantially increasing their sugar content and acidity, adding glycerol (that luscious, syrupy feel in the mouth) and a host of new flavors. It is not as easy it sounds. If it attacks the grapes before they are ripe, or when the weather is too wet, the grapes rot on the vine. And when the climate does conspire (moist, misty mornings followed by warm, sunny afternoons), the resulting juice is in short supply. The grapes also have to be picked by hand, and because they don't all ripen together in this way, countless trips back and forth to the vineyard are required.

The grapes are then crushed and pressed and yeast added, followed by a slow fermentation. The wine is then put into stainless steel, or oak, and left for a few months, before being stabilized, fined and filtered, and, finally, bottled.

The best botrytized wines come from Sauternes and Monbazillac in Bordeaux in good vintages; from Alsace, labeled as *Séléction de Grains Nobles*; Germany's *Trockenbeerenauslese* and *Beerenauslese*; from Austria's Burgenland; from in and around Tokaji in Hungary; plus a line-up of special bottlings from all over the world. Some producers (in California particularly) pick the grapes first then spray them with botrytis spores in the winery to mimic these conditions. The resulting wines can be pretty impressive.

The rest

Some sweet wines are sweet just because they are made with ultra-ripe grapes, and are called late harvest wines. Fruitier-tasting varieties are usually used, such as Riesling.

The grapes are crushed and pressed in a cold stainless steel tank. Yeast is added, then the wine is chilled to stop fermentation (before the sugar has all turned to alcohol), stabilized, fined, filtered, and bottled. Sweet Jurançon is made like this, as are cheaper Sauternes and other sweet whites from the southwest of France in less exceptional vintages, and Germany's Spätlese and Auslese wines, to name a few.

Other sweet wines are made by drying out the grapes on trays, sometimes in hot sunshine, to concentrate the grape's natural sweetness. This method is particularly big in northeast Italy, and the wines are called Recioto (or Amarone, if it's dry).

The most delectable of all is ice wine (or Eiswein). The grapes are only picked when frozen on the vine (a precarious task); when pressed they release a sugar-rich syrup, leaving the frozen water behind in crystals. Canada makes good ice wine, as do Germany and Austria, when the climate is right. Warmer climates have tried with some success, freezing grapes after picking.

above Trebbiano and Malvasia grapes are dried to concentrate their natural sweetness.

far left In the vineyard of Château d'Yquem, the grapes are picked by hand as they do not rot—nobly—simultaneously.

How Fortified Wines are Made

left Tawny port is aged in barrels for six years or more before blending and bottling.

If you add alcohol at a later stage, when fermentation has finished and the sugar has gone, the fortified wine will end up dry. What happens after this depends on the style being made: from port and Madeira, right through to Marsala, Málaga, Australian Liqueur Muscats, and sherry. Let's look at two of the great fortifieds.

Port

Take port. There's nowhere quite like the hot, dry Douro valley, in northern Portugal. Here, ripe, thick-skinned red grapes such as Touriga Nacional are turned into deep, sweet, strong wines made in many different styles. There are two basic categories: those aged in bottle and those aged in wood. And within these two categories, there are many different styles of port.

Vintage port, for example, starts out as it would for dry table wine. But, then, when there is still a good amount of unfermented sugar left, spirit is added to stop fermentation. The alcohol shoots up and the wine becomes sweet. It's put into oak for a year or so, then bottled, and left for at least ten years before drinking.

Aged Tawny port, on the other hand, is aged before bottling. It's left in barrels for six or more years to turn tawny (brownish-orange) in color, then it's blended with different vintages, for added complexity, before bottling.

Most of us view sherry and other fortified wines as old-fashioned drinks. Well, I've got news for you; there is life for fortified wines beyond the crusty colonel's favorite tipple. And when they're good, they're really good —making some of the most exciting wines in the world.

Fortified wines are just that—fortified by spirit. The extra alcohol has two effects: it kills the yeasts and stops fermentation, making the wine higher in alcohol. If you add alcohol before fermentation is finished, while there is still unfermented sugar in the juice, the fortified wine will end up sweet.

Many winemakers in similarly hot climates try their hand at making port-style wines—particularly in Australia, South Africa, and California—but few use the traditional port varieties. The closest to port proper is Banyuls and Maury made in Roussillon, in the south of France.

Sherry

The sherry decanter has got a lot to answer for. The stale contents have turned off many a sherry virgin. But if they'd tried it fresh, they might very well have been smitten—like I was. There are two basic styles of sherry: pale, delicate fino and manzanilla; and dark nutty amontillado and oloroso.

The sherry region is one of the hottest fine wine regions in the world, just across from the coast of North Africa, in southern Spain. The Palomino grape rules here, and so does *flor*—the natural yeast that forms on the surface of the fino when in barrel. That's what gives the wine its unusual tang. When it has matured near the sea, as it is in Sanlúcar de Barrameda's manzanilla, the tang is even more pronounced.

Oloroso starts in the same way as these bone-dry sherries, but more fortifying alcohol is added before it is put into barrel. *Flor* is not encouraged though, and it spends years in barrel, darkening to a deep brown color, with concentrated, spicy wood flavors. It can be bottled dry or sweetened by the addition of concentrated grape juice. If you forget the years in barrel, but do the rest, you get cream sherry, oloroso's much cheaper cousin.

And we mustn't forget the unique solera system, essential to the production of many fortifieds, now used the world over. It's a kind of blending that producers use to keep their product consistent. Imagine a pyramid of barrels of different ages, with the oldest wine on the bottom layer and the youngest wine at the top. Every year, a bit of the wine from the bottom is taken away to be bottled and replaced by wine from the layer above, which is replaced by wine from the layer above that—and so on, until the top layer, which is filled with the current vintage. Clever, eh? Stick this lot in a hot, humid loft on the island of Madeira, and you've got, surprise, surprise—Madeira.

below Far from being relics of a bygone age, fortified wines are among the most exciting. Port and sherry are the two great classics, but there are others.

Wine and Health

Wine—particularly red wine—is good for you. Isn't that just the best news? Scientists have been telling us this, repeatedly, over the last ten years. But we've been drinking wine for centuries, so why now?

It was Prohibition in the US that helped to kick-start the last century of research. Conclusion: moderate consumption of red wine can help prevent heart disease.

It was called the French Paradox: the French indulge in much food and drink with no apparent ill effects on their coronary health. Red wine consumption was cited as a possible factor in reducing the risk of heart disease. After this was aired on US television in 1991, red wine sales went through the roof. Then Asia caught on and witnessed its own wine boom.

Now, there's a mass of evidence that those who drink moderately are less likely to develop and die from coronary heart disease—the Western world's major killer—than either those that drink heavily or those who have never drunk alcohol.

How wine helps

Alcohol, apparently, moderates the level of inflammatory blood chemicals that adversely affect blood cholesterol and blood-clotting proteins. Moderate consumption improves the balance between the harmful and beneficial forms of cholesterol. But alcohol isn't the only factor here. Red wine especially, much more than white wine, is rich in phenolics (the pigment and tannins), which have antioxidant properties. And it is this antioxidant activity that is likely (though it hasn't been conclusively proven yet) to contribute to the heart-protective effects of wine.

How much is moderation?

The million-dollar question. Too much and your behavior changes, your liver is damaged, you're hooked, you cause accidents, and your brain starts to go. Not to mention the link alcohol dependency has to strokes, elevated blood pressure, cancer, infertility, and the rest.

But with moderation it can lift the spirits, aid digestion, prevent heart disease, lower blood pressure, stimulate appetite and even add to your diet—Mediterranean-style, of course.

Just to confuse things, different countries have laid down different rules for "sensible drinking." A "unit" of alcohol in one country is different to a "unit" in another. And there is huge variation between how many can safely be consumed. In the US, for example, the national standard unit of alcohol is 14 g, while its British counterpart contains only 8 g—in Australia, it's 10 g. That's about a small glass of wine, a very small glass of fortified wine, a shot of spirits, or a glass of beer. The French recommend a daily alcohol intake of 60 g for men, while the Brits recommend less than half this amount. And no, it's not okay to save your weekly allowance to drink all in one go: you will be temporarily over-anticoagulated, as a doctor would say, so that you're at an increased risk of stroke.

This is only a rough guide, of course. Age, build, and health must also be taken into account, so common sense must prevail—nothing the Ancient Greeks didn't know about already.

below Moderation is the keynote, but wine is now thought to be beneficial to health. The alcohol helps reduce cholesterol levels in the blood and red wine has antioxidant properties which may protect against heart disease.

A Wine Education

Going to wine school has never been so easy. There are many courses held up and down the country, aimed at all levels of expertise. As well as learning about wine tasting techniques and general wine appreciation, you'll get an introduction to winemaking and vine growing. You might even get a certificate to hang up on your wall.

Schools and Courses

Vindianapolis Associates
Tel: 317.845.0944
golandod@msn.com.

The Italian Culinary Institute
230 Fifth Avenue, Suite 1100
New York, NY 10001
Tel: 212.725.8764
www.italiancookingandliving.com

City College of San Francisco
50 Phelan Avenue
San Francisco, CA 94112
Tel: 415.239.3000

Chicago Wine School
2001 S. Halsted Street, # 100
Chicago, Il 606608
Tel: 312.266.WINE
www.wineschool.com

The Court of Master Sommeliers, American Chapter
1200 Jefferson Street
Napa, CA 94559
Tel: 707.255.7667
courtofms@aol.com

The Culinary Institute of America
Greystone
St. Helena, CA
Tel: 800.333.WCIA
www.ciachef.edu

The Grapes of Path: A Wine School
Tel: 415.701.7335
www.grapesofpath.com
grapesofpath@mindspring.com

The International Wine Academy
38 Portola Drive
San Francisco, CA 94131
Tel: 415.641.4767
www.wineacademy.com
ayoung@firstworld.net

Pacific Rim Wine Education Center
601 Fourth Street, # 103
San Francisco, CA 94107
Tel: 415.512.9318
www.pacrimwine.org
fannie@pacrimwine.org

The International Wine Center
1133 Broadway, Suite 520
New York, NY 10010
Tel: 212.627.7170

Society of Wine Educators
1200, G Street, NW, Suite 360
Washington DC 20005
Tel: 202.347.5677
wine.gurus.com

The Sommelier Society of America, Inc.
PO Box 20080, West Village Station
New York, NY 10014
Tel: 212.679.4190

Sonoma County Wine & Visitors Center
5000 Roberts Lake Road
Rohnert Park, CA
Tel: 707.586.3795

University of Utah
Department of Continuing Education
Salt Lake City, UT 84112
Tel: 801.581.7200

Mendocino College Community Extension
10005 Parallel Drive
Lakeport, CA 95453
Tel: 707.263.4944

Tom Cannavan's On Line Wine Course
www.wine-pages.com/course1.htm

Glossary

Acidity
Acid is naturally present in grapes. Too much and it makes the wine taste too sharp, too little and the wine tastes flabby.

Appellation
A geographically defined wine region. In France, where the word originated, the *appellation contrôlée* system guarantees that a wine comes from where the label says it does, is made from specific grapes, and is produced in a certain way.

Botrytis
Or *Botrytis cinerea* to give it its proper name. An airborne fungus that attacks grapes in cool, humid conditions. Also known as noble rot. It makes them shrivel and rot, concentrating their sugars and flavors.

Carbonic maceration
Fermentation that occurs inside intact red grapes —particularly the Gamay grape in Beaujolais, France—producing purple, fruity wines for drinking young.

Chaptalization
Adding of sugar during fermentation to raise a wine's alcoholic strength.

Classed growth (or cru classé in French)
A vineyard, estate, or château included in the Bordeaux wine classification system. In 1855, 61 red wines of the Médoc (plus one from the Graves) were classified as cru classé, and divided into five ranks determined by price. Just a handful more have been classified since.

Corked
That damp, musty smell you get sometimes, when the cork is diseased and taints the taste and smell of the wine.

Cru
French word for "growth," used to refer to the wine of an individual vineyard.

Cuvée
French term for a blended wine or a special selection.

Domaine
A wine estate, particularly in Burgundy.

Dosage
The final addition to a sparkling wine that may top up a bottle in the case of Champagne method wines, and also determines the sweetness of the finished wine.

Enologist
A wine scientist.

En primeur
The wine-trade term for wine sold as futures, common practice with wines from Bordeaux.

Fining and filtering
People don't really want murky-looking wines, so small particles are removed. This is done by adding an agent to the wine which absorbs said particles and sinks to the bottom, before being removed. Common agents include egg whites, dried ox blood, bentonite clay, and isinglass. The wine is then passed through a fine filter.

Flying winemaker
Or "international winemaker." Wineries the world over recruit the services of consultant winemakers to improve their wines.

Hybrid
Grape bred from an American vine species and European Vitis vinifera.

Late-harvest
Late-harvest grapes contain more sugar and concentrated flavors, and are therefore usually sweet.

Lees
All the gunk that falls to the bottom of a tank— dead yeast cells, bits of pulp, seeds, stalks. Also refers to the dead yeast cells that fall to the bottom of the bottle of bubbly after its secondary fermentation.

Malolactic fermentation
This can take place in newly fermented wine where crisp, hard malic acid is converted by bacteria to much softer, lactic acid. It can happen on its own, but is usually induced by the winemaker.

Mousse
A good sparkling wine should have a mousse that stays in the glass and ideally the bubbles should be as small as possible.

Négociant
French word for a merchant or shipper who buys wine or grapes from growers, then matures, and sometimes blends the wine, before bottling and selling.

New World
Every wine-producing country other than Europe, basically. It's a state of mind too, as the so-called New World producers tend to keep pace better with new technology.

Noble rot
see "Botrytis"

Old World
The traditional wine-producing countries of Europe, such as France, Spain, Italy, and Germany (although it includes the UK too). They generally use more traditional techniques in their wine making.

Old vines
The older the vine the better, in terms of quality wine production.

Oxidation
Expose wine to air and it goes brown and flat, eventually turning into vinegar. Though used in a controlled way—in the production of sherry, for example—it can make the wine more complex.

Phylloxera
The scourge of the wine world. This vine-root-munching louse swept through Europe and elsewhere at the end of the nineteenth century. Consequently, vines are now invariably grafted onto more resistant American rootstocks.

Quaffing
Glugging wines to knock back—not think about too much. Easy, fruity, good-value quaffers.

Rootstock
The root stump of the vine on to which the fruiting branches are grafted.

Sulfur
Used during vinification for cleaning equipment; as an antioxidant with fresh grapes and wine; added as sulfur dioxide to stop or to delay fermentation.

Sur lie
French term for "on the lees," applied to white wines that derive a bit more character from some form of lees contact.

Tannin
The same mouth-coating feeling you get from a mug of road-mender's tea, tannins are found in grape skins and stalks. Red wines are usually high in tannin if they are made from grapes with thick skins, or have had a long maceration or contact with stalks during fermentation. Tannins also seep out of oak barrels into the wine.

Terroir
A great catchall French word that refers to the type of soil, climate, drainage, and position of a vineyard.

Varietal
Wine made from, and named after, a single grape variety.

Vinification
The process of turning grapes into wine.

Vintage
The harvest, and the term given to a wine of a particular year.

Viticulture
Vine-growing and vineyard management.

Yield
Important factor in determining the quality of wine. The less grapes there are on the vine, the more concentrated the juice, and the wine.

Index

Acknowledgements

Special thanks go to Susan Low for her help
and to St. Martin Vintners Ltd., Brighton, UK.

The publishers would like to thank Hanningtons, Brighton, UK.
for the use of properties.

The publishers would like to thank the following
for the use of photographs:

CEPHAS Picture Library: 9, 10, 14, 15, 16, 17, 18, 20, 21 (top left), 22, 23, 25, 26, 29, 30, 33, 37, 66, 72, 73 (top & bottom), 84, 85, 88, 91, 93, 94 (top left), 95, 96, 97, 98 (top & bottom left), 99 (center & bottom left), 101 (top & bottom), 102 (top & bottom), 103 (top and bottom left), 105, 106 (top), 107 (top, middle and bottom left), 109, 110 (top), 111 (top & bottom left), 113, 114 (top & bottom), 115 (top & bottom left), 117 (top & bottom), 119 (top & bottom), 120 (top & bottom), 121, 122, 123, 125 (top & bottom), 126 (top & bottom), 127 (top & bottom left), 129 (top), 130, 131 (top & bottom), 133 (top & middle), 135, 136, 137, 139, 140 (bottom), 141 (top & bottom), 143 (top & bottom), 145, 146, 148, 149 (top & bottom), 150, 151, 152, 153, 154, 155 (top & bottom), 156, 157, 158, 159, 160 (top & bottom), 161, 162, 163, 164, 165, 166

Image Bank 40, 41 (bottom), 42, 64

Tony Stone 34, 45 (bottom), 78, 169

Superstock 7, 168

Elizabeth Whiting Associates 87